Civil Disobedience and Violence

Basic Problems in Philosophy Series

A. I. Melden and Stanley Munsat
University of California, Irvine
General Editors

Civil Disobedience and Violence

Edited by

Jeffrie G. Murphy

The University of Arizona

Wadsworth Publishing Company, Inc. Belmont, California

Dedicated to my Mother and to the memory of my Father

Creon: . . . To transgress
Or twist the law to one's own pleasure, presume
To order where one should obey, is sinful,
And I will have none of it.
He whom the State appoints must be obeyed
To the smallest matter, be it right—or wrong. . . .

Antigone: . . . That order did not come from God. Justice,
That dwells with the gods below, knows no such law.
I did not think your edicts strong enough
To overrule the unwritten unalterable laws
Of God and heaven, you being only a man. . . .

Sophocles, *Antigone*

From Sophocles, *The Theban Plays,* translated by E. F. Watling,
Penguin Edition, London, 1947, pp. 144 and 138.

L. C. Cat. Card No.: 78–158119
ISBN: 0–534–0051–7

Printed in the United States of America

2 3 4 5 6 7 8 9 10—75 74 73 72

Series Foreword

The Basic Problems in Philosophy Series is designed to meet the need of students and teachers of philosophy, mainly but not exclusively at the undergraduate level, for collections of essays devoted to some fairly specific philosophical problems.

In recent years there have been numerous paperback collections on a variety of philosophical topics. Those teachers who wish to refer their students to a set of essays on a specific philosophical problem have usually been frustrated, however, since most of these collections range over a wide set of issues and problems. The present series attempts to remedy this situation by presenting together, within each volume, key writings on a single philosophical issue.

Given the magnitude of the literature, there can be no thought of completeness. Rather, the materials included are those that, in the judgment of the editor, must be mastered first by the student who wishes to acquaint himself with relevant issues and their ramifications. To this end, historical as well as contemporary writings are included.

Each volume in the series contains an introduction by the editor to set the stage for the arguments contained in the essays and a bibliography to help the student who wishes to pursue the topic at a more advanced level.

A. I. Melden
S. Munsat

Jeffrie G. Murphy is an Associate Professor of Philosophy at the University of Arizona. He received a B.A. degree from Johns Hopkins University and a Ph.D. from the University of Rochester. During the academic year 1968–69 he was awarded a fellowship from the National Endowment for the Humanities for a year of study at the School of Law, University of California, Los Angeles. He has taught at the University of Minnesota, the University of Michigan, and the University of California, Los Angeles. He has published a book, *Kant: The Philosophy of Right* (1970), and several articles, including "Allegiance and Lawful Government" (*Ethics,* October, 1968) and "Criminal Punishment and Psychiatric Fallacies" (*Law and Society Review,* August, 1969). He is currently serving as chairman of the Arizona Civil Liberties Union Committee on Psychiatric Justice.

Contents

Introduction

Civil disobedience, unlike many other practical problems of
importance, has received a great deal of attention from philosophers, legal scholars, and political theorists. Thus the selections that I have included in this collection represent but a
small sample of the writings that are available on the topic.
Their purpose is not to settle, once and for all, the difficult
problems raised by the topic of civil disobedience. Rather the
aim of the collection is much more modest: to acquaint the
reader with the important issues and to provide him with some
background and beginning tools for thinking these issues
through for himself. For the most part, I have tried to select essays relevant to evaluating civil disobedience in the context of
contemporary American democracy.

What is civil disobedience? This is itself a philosophical
question, and it is one about which there has been much disagreement. Most, however, would agree that the following are
at least *necessary* conditions for analyzing or defining "civil
disobedience": An act *A* is properly called an act of civil disobedience only if (1) there is some law *L* according to which *A*
is illegal, (2) *L* is believed by the agent to be immoral, unconstitutional, irreligious, or ideologically objectionable, and (3)
this belief about *L* motivates or explains the performance of *A*.[1]
It is of crucial importance here to distinguish the civil disobedient from the criminal disobedient and from the revolutionary. The revolutionary has a different *end* from that of the
civil disobedient. The latter objects to particular laws or policies but has fidelity to the system as a whole. The former has

---

[1] Two qualifications need to be noted concerning this analysis. (1) The
agent may have no objection to *L per se* but may violate *L* because he views
it as symbolic for or instrumentally involved with some other law *L'* (or some
general policy *P*) to which he does object. In my view, such a person (Thoreau for example) is also to be regarded as civilly disobedient. (2) The line
between moral, constitutional, religious and ideological motives is not an
easy one to draw. Also, more than one of these motives may be involved
in explaining a particular case of civil disobedience. What is most important
is that motives of this sort be distinguished from the typical criminal motive:
self-interest. We do not think of a criminal act as a *public* act of *protest;*
but these features *do* typically characterize acts of civil disobedience.

no such fidelity and wants to overthrow the system entirely.[2] The civil disobedient differs from the criminal primarily in terms of *motive*. The ordinary criminal may be viewed as acting primarily out of motives of self-interest—motives which render him morally blameworthy and socially dangerous. Though the civil disobedient violates penal statutes (and so in one clear sense *is* a criminal), he differs so markedly from the paradigm criminal (in terms of motives, moral blameworthiness, danger to society, etc.) that to classify him merely as "criminal" would be to blur some important distinctions and to miss some important moral problems—for example, the problem of how society ought to respond to him.

Now few would consider the conditions I have listed as controversial if they are regarded merely as necessary conditions for civil disobedience. Many, however, would argue that by themselves these conditions are not sufficient—that other conditions must be satisfied before we have a true case of civil disobedience. And here we enter dangerous conceptual territory. For it is unfortunately common for philosophers to build their own moral preferences into definitions, to try to solve substantive moral issues by stipulation. Thus civil disobedience may be defined in such a way that it is necessarily justified. Or it may be defined so as to logically require the acceptance of punishment or to logically require the use of nonviolent means. But such definitions may beg important questions of moral substance. Surely an act can properly be called an act of civil disobedience even if it is unjustified. And the question whether the civil disobedient must accept his punishment or the question whether he must avoid violence seem to me morally open questions. We make the matter appear too easy if we try to solve problems like these with definitions.[3]

---

[2] There can, of course, be borderline cases here. Some civil disobedients (pacifists and civil rights activists) have objected to large segments of law. And the question of exactly how much one must object to in order to be considered an objector to the system as a whole is not susceptible of an exact answer. Also some revolutionaries (such as Gandhi) may employ civil disobedience as a *tactic* and some (such as the Founding Fathers) may genuinely object only to a few laws. In spite of these difficulties, however, I think it is helpful to view those cases in which the end sought is *not* the total overthrow of the government as the paradigm of civil disobedience. The Founding Fathers, though their real objection was only to a few laws, were still revolutionaries because they believed that the only way to change these laws was by an overthrow of the existing government.

[3] It is extremely common for writers to confuse the problem of defining civil disobedience with the problem of justifying it, to regard civil disobedience as justified law violation. But this is a mistake. Acts of civil disobedience may be unjustified, and justified acts of law violation may not be acts of civil disobedience. Consider the following two cases: (1) Lester Maddox violating integration law and barring blacks from his restaurant and (2) an individual driving over the speed limit in order to get a critically

By way of illustration, let us briefly consider the connection between civil disobedience and the acceptance of punishment.[4] It has often been suggested that the civilly disobedient individual is *logically,* and not just morally, required to openly accept his punishment. To say that he is logically required is to say not merely that it is morally right for him to accept it, but that the term "civil disobedient" is not properly applied to him if he does not. Two reasons can be given in defense of this claim. First, it is conceptually important to distinguish the civil disobedient from the mere criminal. One way to do this is to argue that criminals flee their punishments whereas civil disobedients embrace theirs. Second, the civilly disobedient individual, unlike the revolutionary, respects the legal system as a whole but objects to particular laws. His disobedience testifies to his particular objection; his willingness to accept the legally prescribed punishment testifies to his general fidelity to the system as a whole.

I do not myself find either of these arguments convincing. It is plausible to maintain that what distinguishes the civil disobedient from the mere criminal is a motivational difference. Now willingness to accept punishment certainly provides *evidence* that one has a noncriminal motive, but it is surely possible that such a motive could be established on other grounds —such as past actions, statements, and religious upbringing. Thus I should argue that the connection between acceptance

---

injured child to the hospital. In the former, we have an act of civil disobedience (assuming Maddox's motives were in fact as he described them) which was in my view unjustified. In the latter, we have a justified act of law violation which (since no protest was involved) could hardly be called an act of civil disobedience. This confusion of definition with justification appears even in Gandhi's famous definition of civil disobedience as a "civil breach of unmoral statutory enactments" (*Non-Violent Resistance* [New York, 1964], p. 3). He could have improved his definition considerably by speaking, not of unmoral enactments, but of enactments *believed* by the agent to be unmoral. This would leave open the possibility for error on the part of the civil disobedient, and it is important to do this. Conscience, alas, is not an infallible guide to action. For the claim that civil disobedience logically requires the acceptance of punishment, see John Rawls, "The Justification of Civil Disobedience," in *Civil Disobedience: Theory and Practice,* ed. Hugo Adam Bedau (New York, 1969), p. 247. For the claim that civil disobedience logically requires nonviolence, see Hugo Adam Bedau, "On Civil Disobedience," *Journal of Philosophy,* Vol. LVIII, No. 21 (1961), pp. 656, 661. What is really at issue here is whether "civil disobedience" should be understood as a term of moral approbation. My view is that it facilitates moral debate to treat the term as morally neutral. Since the term has been bandied about so much in recent years, there is no standard meaning for it. Thus we must choose a meaning, and our criterion for choice should be whatever clarifies and facilitates debate on the topic. Morally loaded definitions do neither.

[4] The logical relationship between civil disobedience and violence is discussed in this book in the essays by Christian Bay and Howard Zinn. Those who claim that civil disobedience logically requires nonviolence very often commit the following fallacy: believing that since civil disobedience and violence are logically distinct they are therefore logically incompatible.

of punishment and civil disobedience is a *contingent evidential* connection and not a logically necessary connection. Similarly with the problem of fidelity to the legal system. Acceptance of punishment provides evidence of fidelity, but it is logically possible that fidelity could be established in some other way. Indeed, one might be so loyal to the Constitution that he would not accept punishment under a statute which, in his judgment, violates the Constitution—even if the Supreme Court has upheld the statute's constitutional validity. The Court can make mistakes of interpretation, after all, and loyalty to the Constitution is not the same as loyalty to the Court.

Against the claim that civil disobedience logically requires the acceptance of punishment, it is also worth noting the following. The question "Should the civil disobedient accept his punishment?" seems to make perfectly good sense. Indeed, Plato devotes the whole dialogue *Crito* to reporting Socrates' answer to this question. If it were a logical truth or a truth of language that the civil disobedient accepts his punishment, however, it would be pointless to raise such a question. This would be like conducting an inquiry into the question "I wonder if there are any unmarried bachelors?" But the question of punishment for civil disobedience does not seem like this at all, and so in my judgment it is premature to close off moral discussion by regarding it as logically true that the civil disobedient accepts his punishment. If he must accept his punishment, I should want to regard this as a *moral* (and not a logical) "must"—a "must" that will have to be supported (as Socrates tries to support it) with moral argumentation. Obviously it is morally important that the civil disobedient demonstrate his sincerity and his fidelity, and accepting punishment is one good way to do this. Thus we might even say that the civil disobedient has a *prima facie* moral obligation to accept his punishment. But this leaves open the possibility that, in particular cases, strong moral reasons may weigh against such acceptance and that these reasons may override. Even considerations of self-interest may be relevant if the legally prescribed punishment is of a severity out of all reasonable proportion to the gravity of the offense. It is also worth considering whether an individual who believes that he is an important member of a protest movement, the goals of which he believes to be morally and politically important, might not reasonably choose to avoid punishment so as not thereby to weaken the movement. Civil disobedience, whether we like it or not, is in fact a way of mobilizing power for certain social goals. And thus civil disobedients will often and quite naturally consider, in making their decisions, the likely effect of their actions on their ability to mobilize power of the right sort.

To avoid begging any important questions, then, I propose that the conditions I have previously listed as necessary for civil disobedience be regarded (with the noted qualifications) as also jointly sufficient. (An act A is properly called an act of civil disobedience if and only if (1) there is some law L according to which A is illegal, (2) L is believed by the agent to be immoral, unconstitutional, irreligious or ideologically objectionable, and (3) this belief about L motivates or explains the performance of A.) This provides us with at least a provisional definition of civil disobedience as a background for the readings in this collection.[5]

The following essays, though some contain attempts at defining civil disobedience, are mainly concerned with problems of evaluation and justification. Following the classic statements by Socrates and Thoreau, the essay by John Rawls (using a sophisticated elaboration of the "social contract" argument put forth by Socrates) explores the general topic of the moral obligation to obey the law. This is the topic with which any discussion of civil disobedience has to begin; for if there is in general no obligation to obey the law, there is no special *problem* of civil disobedience. It is only because we typically believe that the burden of moral proof lies with the disobedient— that he (and not the law-abiding citizen) must justify his conduct—that we seek for theories of justification for civil disobedience.

Rawls' essay on the obligation to obey the law is followed by three essays on the justification for civil disobedience. Two essays are concerned with the circumstances in which individuals may be said to have a moral right to engage in civil disobedience. Sidney Hook, though a strong opponent of civil disobedience in contemporary America, believes that it is possible for circumstances to arise (as they have in the past) in which civil disobedience might be legitimate. He is concerned, however, to lay down careful rules governing the *form* that civil disobedience must take in order not to lose its legitimacy even in such circumstances. He argues, for example, that justified civil disobedience is always nonviolent. He also argues that one may rightfully engage in civil disobedience only if all

---

[5] It should be clear that it is simpleminded to characterize, as opponents of civil disobedience are often inclined to do, acts of civil disobedience as acts of "breaking laws one doesn't like." Of course a reasonable man would find it difficult to approve of an act so described; but, as the above analysis indicates, acts of civil disobedience are not to be so simply described.

legal channels for change are clearly closed. In my essay, I outline conditions under which one may claim a right to disobey
the law, and I attempt to present a *prima facie* case that, with
respect to draft resistance against the war in Vietnam, these
conditions have been satisfied. I argue, among other things,
that there is evidence that the legal channels Hook speaks of
have been, for all practical purposes, closed. The next essay,
by Christian Bay, is an attempt to set out conditions under
which individuals may be said not merely to have a right to
disobey, but to have good and perhaps sufficient moral-politi-
cal reasons for disobeying—that is, conditions under which it
is not merely morally *permissible* for them to break the law but
under which they (at least *prima facie*) *ought* to break it. Bay
develops his argument by stressing the importance of loyalty
to the *values* and *ideals* that democracy is supposed to serve
rather than loyalty to the mere forms of democracy.

These essays on justification are followed by two discussions of civil disobedience and violence.[6] (This topic is also
explored at the end of Bay's article.) Against violent disobedience, Mohandas K. Gandhi suggests the following: that violence degrades and brutalizes the man who uses it and that no
man, given that his beliefs are subject to error, should be so
presumptuous as to inflict harm on others in furtherance of
those beliefs. And to those who say that nonviolence does not
work as a tactic, Gandhi asks the following questions. Has
nonviolence ever been given an adequate test? Have we ever
even seriously considered pouring into techniques of nonviolence the money and energy and patience that we now pour
into techniques of destruction?

Howard Zinn, though himself suspicious of violence as a
tactic, believes that it cannot be ruled out as *a priori* unjustified. Violence (as both Zinn and Bay stress) may be institu-
tionalized in certain social and legal arrangements; so it may
not always be possible to avoid its presence and damaging
consequences. Thus (though we should be *very* cautious in
making such a judgment) the use of violence against already
violent institutions may, in the long run, reduce the amount of

---

[6] The proper analysis of the meaning of "violence" is philosophically
controversial. The reader might consult Newton Garver's "What Violence
Is" (*Nation*, June 24, 1968) and J. M. Cameron's "On Violence" (*New York
Review of Books*, July 2, 1970). There is also an excellent study by Robert L.
Holmes, "Violence and Nonviolence," which will appear in *Violence*, ed.
Jerome Shaffer (New York, 1971). Holmes' essay was one of the winning
essays in competition sponsored by the Council for Philosophical Studies
on the topic "violence." The other winning essay, "Violence and the Rule
of Law" by Bernard Harrison, will also appear in this volume.

violence in the world.[7] The advocate of political violence, then, is often concerned to argue that we are morally responsible for our omissions as well as for our commissions. If we claim to abhor violence, can we be satisfied merely with not doing any violence ourselves? If we really abhor it, might we not want to oppose (with some violence if necessary) those institutions which promote violence? If we do not effectively oppose such institutions, is it clear that (considering such omissions) we are free of moral responsibility for the remaining institution-alized violence? Is it clear that we are any less morally guilty than had we actually committed acts of violence? The reader must determine for himself the extent to which the Gandhian doctrine of nonviolence can be defended against these worries.

Following these discussions of civil disobedience and violence, the essay by Ronald Dworkin explores the question "How should government respond to the civilly disobedient individual?" This question is extremely important and yet has not drawn nearly the attention that it deserves. And, as Dworkin argues, it is a much more subtle and complex question than one might at first suppose—in part because the legal issues involved are subtle and complex.

The collection concludes with an essay by the anarchist Peter Kropotkin. All the previous writers (with the possible exception of Thoreau) appear to share the belief that in general all citizens have an obligation to obey the law, that any disobedience must be justified by overriding moral considerations. The underlying assumption here is that government, with its rule of law, provides essential benefits to its citizens and that, to retain these benefits, citizens must generally obey the law. In common with Marxist writers, Kropotkin argues that talk of a just rule of law, no matter how fine it sounds in theory, functions in actual societies as a rhetorical mask for exploitation and class privilege. He denies the assumption that the rule of law provides benefits sufficient to outweigh the oppression of its coercive power and thus denies that there is even in general any obligation to obey the law. Thus, if Kropotkin is right, there is no special problem of civil disobedience; for

[7] It is important to note that the question whether violence is effective is an empirical question and not a question of moral principle. Gandhi believes that using violence is not an effective way to reduce the amount of violence in the world, but he also typically appeals to moral principles which would condemn violence even if it were effective. For a philosophical attack on such principles, see Jan Narveson's "Pacifism: A Philosophical Analysis," *Ethics*, July 1965.

civil disobedience does not even *prima facie* stand in need of justification. It is rather *obedience* which needs to be justified![8]

It is hoped that the wide variety of opinions presented in these essays will stimulate the reader to further thought on the topics raised. We have all witnessed a great deal of poltiical action in recent years, but very little in the way of political thought. And a rational man, whatever his own political ideology, must find this deeply troublesome. As action precedes thought, so does barbarism replace civilization.

I should like to express my thanks to Ronald Milo for valuable discussions on the topic of civil disobedience and to Charles Ares, Mitchell Axler, and Winton Woods for their helpful suggestions concerning the anthology. Marcella Brady and Kay Lane helped in the preparation of the manuscript, and my wife Nancy aided me in the correction of the proofs. I am very grateful to them all.

[8] I have not included an essay by a Communist writer because, being revolutionaries, Communists tend to think in terms broader than those of mere civil disobedience. If they talk about the problem at all, they tend to argue that civil disobedience is justified only in so far as it is an initial tactic in revolution. If it is not such a tactic, it is viewed as a bourgeois self-indulgence which (especially if coupled with a belief in nonviolence) provides a harmless safety valve for a system that ought to explode. See "Pacifism and Violence: A Study in Bourgeois Ethics" by Christopher Caudwell in his *Studies and Further Studies in a Dying Culture* (New York, 1938). John Locke, another revolutionary theorist, also made no place for civil disobedience in his theory.

Socrates

On Disobeying the Law

From *Apology*

. . . *Socrates.* . . . I have said enough in answer to the charge of Meletus:[1] any elaborate defence is unnecessary; but I know only too well how many are the enmities which I have incurred, and this is what will be my destruction if I am destroyed;—not Meletus, nor yet Anytus, but the envy and detraction of the world, which has been the death of many good men, and will probably be the death of many more; there is no danger of my being the last of them.

Some one will say: And are you not ashamed, Socrates, of a course of life which is likely to bring you to an untimely end? To him I may fairly answer: There you are mistaken: a man who is good for anything ought not to calculate the chance of living or dying; he ought only to consider whether in doing anything he is doing right or wrong—acting the part of a good man or of a bad. Whereas, upon your view, the heroes who fell at Troy were not good for much, and the son of Thetis above all, who altogether despised danger in comparison with disgrace; and

These selections (abridged) are from Benjamin Jowett's translations (1892) of Plato's *Apology* and *Crito*. Scholars generally agree that these dialogues, though written by Plato (approx. 428–348 B.C.), are primarily reports of the conversations of his teacher Socrates (approx. 470–399 B.C.) on the topics of civil disobedience and the acceptance of punishment. In *Apology*, Socrates, who has been charged with impiety and corrupting the youth with his teaching of philosophy, presents his defense and, after conviction, his response to the sentence of death imposed by the court. He argues that he is bound by a divine law that is higher than state law to publicly pursue the truth and that he would not desist from doing this even if ordered to do so by the state. In *Crito*, Socrates presents his arguments (one being the earliest known version of the social contract theory) in support of his view that he owes a duty of fidelity to the state. He argues that, because of this duty, it would be wrong for him to escape his legal punishment even though he knows that his conviction was unjust. For an excellent discussion of the ideas in these two dialogues, see A. D. Woozley's "Socrates on Disobeying the Law," forthcoming in *Socrates,* ed. Gregory Vlastos (New York: Doubleday).

[1] [Meletus and Anytus are Socrates' accusers. Ed.]

when he was so eager to slay Hector, his goddess mother said to him, that if he avenged his companion, Patroclus, and slew Hector, he would die himself—'Fate,' she said, in these or the like words, 'waits for you next after Hector;' he, receiving this warning, utterly despised danger and death, and instead of fearing them, feared rather to live in dishonour, and not to avenge his friend. 'Let me die forthwith,' he replies, 'and be avenged of my enemy, rather than abide here by the beaked ships, a laughing-stock and a burden of the earth.' Had Achilles any thought of death and danger? For wherever a man's place is, whether the place which he has chosen or that in which he has been placed by a commander, there he ought to remain in the hour of danger; he should not think of death or of anything but of disgrace. And this, O men of Athens, is a true saying.

Strange, indeed, would be my conduct, O men of Athens, if I who, when I was ordered by the generals whom you chose to command me at Potidaea and Amphipolis and Delium, remained where they placed me, like any other man, facing death —if now, when, as I conceive and imagine, God orders me to fulfil the philosopher's mission of searching into myself and other men, I were to desert my post through fear of death, or any other fear; that would indeed be strange, and I might justly be arraigned in court for denying the existence of the gods, if I disobeyed the oracle because I was afraid of death, fancying that I was wise when I was not wise. For the fear of death is indeed the pretence of wisdom, and not real wisdom, being a pretence of knowing the unknown; and no one knows whether death, which men in their fear apprehend to be the greatest evil, may not be the greatest good. Is not this ignorance of a disgraceful sort, the ignorance which is the conceit that man knows what he does not know? And in this respect only I believe myself to differ from men in general, and may perhaps claim to be wiser than they are:—that whereas I know but little of the world below, I do not suppose that I know: but I do know that injustice and disobedience to a better, whether God or man, is evil and dishonourable, and I will never fear or avoid a possible good rather than a certain evil. And therefore if you let me go now, and are not convinced by Anytus, who said that since I had been prosecuted I must be put to death (or if not that I ought never to have been prosecuted at all); and that if I escape now, your sons will all be utterly ruined by listening to my words—if you say to me, Socrates, this time we will not mind Anytus, and you shall be let off, but upon one condition, that you are not to enquire and speculate in this way any more, and that if you are caught doing so again you shall die;—if this was the condition on which you let me go, I should reply: Men of Athens, I honour and love you; but I shall obey God rather than you, and while I have life and strength I shall never cease from the practice and teaching of philosophy, exhorting any one whom I meet and saying to him after my manner: You, my friend,—a citizen of the great and mighty and wise city of Athens,—are you not ashamed of heaping up the greatest amount of money and honour and reputation, and caring so little about wisdom and truth and the greatest improvement of the soul, which you never regard or heed at all? And if the person with whom I am arguing, says: Yes, but I do care; then I do not leave him or let him go at once; but I proceed to interrogate and examine and cross-examine him, and if I think that he has no virtue in him, but only says that he has, I reproach him with undervaluing the greater, and overvaluing the less. And I shall repeat the same words to every one whom I meet, young and old, citizen and alien, but especially to the citizens, inasmuch as they are my brethren. For know that this is the command of God; and I believe that no greater good has ever happened in the state than my service to the God. For I do nothing but go about persuading you all, old and young alike, not to take thought for your persons or your properties, but first and chiefly to care about the greatest improvement of the soul. I tell you that virtue is not given by money, but that from virtue comes money and every other good of man, public as well as private. This is my teaching, and if this is the doctrine which corrupts the youth, I am a mischievous person. But if any one says that this is not my teaching, he is speaking an untruth. Wherefore, O men of Athens, I say to you, do as Anytus bids or not as Anytus bids, and either acquit me or not; but whichever you do, understand that I shall never alter my ways, not even if I have to die many times. . . .

Some one may wonder why I go about in private giving advice and busying myself with the concerns of others, but do not venture to come forward in public and advise the state. I will tell you why. You have heard me speak at sundry times and in divers places of an oracle or sign which comes to me, and is the divinity which Meletus ridicules in the indictment. This sign, which is a kind of voice, first began to come to me when I was a child; it always forbids but never commands me to do anything which I am going to do. This is what deters me from being a politician. And rightly, as I think. For I am certain, O men of Athens, that if I had engaged in politics, I should have perished long ago, and done no good either to you or to myself. And do not be offended at my telling you the truth: for the truth is, that no man who goes to war with you or any other multitude, honestly striving against the many lawless and unrighteous deeds which are done in a state, will save his life; he who will fight for the right, if he would live even for a brief space, must have a private station and not a public one. . . .

Some one will say: Yes, Socrates, but cannot you hold your tongue, and then you may go into a foreign city, and no one will interfere with you? Now I have great difficulty in making you understand my answer to this. For if I tell you that to do as you say would be a disobedience to the God, and therefore that I cannot hold my tongue, you will not believe that I am serious; and if I say again that daily to discourse about virtue, and of those other things about which you hear me examining myself and others, is the greatest good of man, and that the unexamined life is not worth living, you are still less likely to believe me. Yet I say what is true, although a thing of which it is hard for me to persuade you. . . .

. . . The difficulty, my friends, is not to avoid death, but to avoid unrighteousness; for that runs faster than death. I am old and move slowly, and the slower runner has overtaken me, and my accusers are keen and quick, and the faster runner, who is unrighteousness, has overtaken them. And now I depart hence condemned by you to suffer the penalty of death,— they too go their ways condemned by the truth to suffer the penalty of villainy and wrong; and I must abide by my award— let them abide by theirs. I suppose that these things may be regarded as fated,—and I think that they are well. . . .

From Crito

. . . *Socrates.* From these premises[2] I proceed to argue the question whether I ought or ought not to try and escape without the consent of the Athenians: and if I am clearly right in escaping, then I will make the attempt; but if not, I will abstain. The other considerations which you mention, of money and loss of character and the duty of educating one's children, are,

[2] [In the earlier part of the dialogue, Crito has offered several arguments to persuade Socrates to escape from prison: escape would allow him to continue philosophizing in another country, would allow him to continue caring for his family, and would save his friends from the condemnation of public opinion as not having been resourceful enough to save their teacher. Socrates replies that he will be moved by neither passion nor appeals to public opinion but only by reason, that he will remain what he "always has been—a man who will accept no argument but that which on reflection I find to be the truest." These are the "premises" on which the following discussion must rest. Ed.]

I fear, only the doctrines of the multitude, who would be as ready to restore people to life, if they were able, as they are to put them to death—and with as little reason. But now, since the argument has thus far prevailed, the only question which remains to be considered is, whether we shall do rightly either in escaping or in suffering others to aid in our escape and paying them in money and thanks, or whether in reality we shall not do rightly; and if the latter, then death or any other calamity which may ensue on my remaining here must not be allowed to enter into the calculation.

Crito. I think that you are right, Socrates; how then shall we proceed?

Soc. Let us consider the matter together, and do you either refute me if you can, and I will be convinced; or else cease, my dear friend, from repeating to me that I ought to escape against the wishes of the Athenians: for I highly value your attempts to persuade me to do so, but I may not be persuaded against my own better judgment. And now please to consider my first position, and try how you can best answer me.

Cr. I will.

Soc. Are we to say that we are never intentionally to do wrong, or that in one way we ought and in another we ought not to do wrong, or is doing wrong always evil and dishonourable, as I was just now saying, and as has been already acknowledged by us? Are all our former admissions which were made within a few days to be thrown away? And have we, at our age, been earnestly discoursing with one another all our life long only to discover that we are no better than children? Or, in spite of the opinion of the many, and in spite of consequences whether better or worse, shall we insist on the truth of what was then said, that injustice is always an evil and dishonour to him who acts unjustly? Shall we say so or not?

Cr. Yes.

Soc. Then we must do no wrong?

Cr. Certainly not.

Soc. Nor when injured injure in return, as the many imagine; for we must injure no one at all?

Cr. Clearly not.

Soc. Again, Crito, may we do evil?

Cr. Surely not, Socrates.

Soc. And what of doing evil in return for evil, which is the morality of the many—is that just or not?

Cr. Not just.

Soc. For doing evil to another is the same as injuring him?

Cr. Very true.

Soć. Then we ought not to retaliate or render evil for evil to any one, whatever evil we may have suffered from him. But I would have you consider, Crito, whether you really mean what you are saying. For this opinion has never been held, and never will be held, by any considerable number of persons; and those who are agreed and those who are not agreed upon this point have no common ground, and can only despise one another when they see how widely they differ. Tell me, then, whether you agree with and assent to my first principle, that neither injury nor retaliation nor warding off evil by evil is ever right. And shall that be the premiss of our argument? Or do you decline and dissent from this? For so I have ever thought, and continue to think; but, if you are of another opinion, let me hear what you have to say. If, however, you remain of the same mind as formerly, I will proceed to the next step.

Cr. You may proceed, for I have not changed my mind.

Soc. Then I will go on to the next point, which may be put in the form of a question:—Ought a man to do what he admits to be right, or ought he to betray the right?

Cr. He ought to do what he thinks right.

Soc. But if this is true, what is the application? In leaving the prison against the will of the Athenians, do I wrong any? or rather do I not wrong those whom I ought least to wrong? Do I not desert the principles which were acknowledged by us to be just—what do you say?

Cr. I cannot tell, Socrates; for I do not know.

Soc. Then consider the matter in this way:—Imagine that I am about to play truant (you may call the proceeding by any name which you like), and the laws and the government come and interrogate me: 'Tell us, Socrates,' they say; 'what are you about? are you not going by an act of yours to overturn us—the laws, and the whole state, as far as in you lies? Do you imagine that a state can subsist and not be overthrown, in which the decisions of law have no power, but are set aside and trampled upon by individuals?' What will be our answer, Crito, to these and the like words? Any one, and especially a rhetorician, will have a good deal to say on behalf of the law which requires a sentence to be carried out. He will argue that this law should not be set aside; and shall we reply, 'Yes; but the state has injured us and given an unjust sentence.' Suppose I say that?

Cr. Very good, Socrates.

Soc. 'And was that our agreement with you?' the law would answer; 'or were you to abide by the sentence of the state?' And if I were to express my astonishment at their words, the

law would probably add: 'Answer, Socrates, instead of opening your eyes—you are in the habit of asking and answering
questions. Tell us,—What complaint have you to make against
us which justifies you in attempting to destroy us and the state?
In the first place did we not bring you into existence? Your
father married your mother by our aid and begat you. Say
whether you have any objection to urge against those of us
who regulate marriage?' None, I should reply. 'Or against those
of us who after birth regulate the nurture and education of children, in which you also were trained? Were not the laws, which
have the charge of education, right in commanding your father
to train you in music and gymnastic?' Right, I should reply.
'Well then, since you were brought into the world and nurtured
and educated by us, can you deny in the first place that you are
our child and slave, as your fathers were before you? And if
this is true you are not on equal terms with us; nor can you
think that you have a right to do to us what we are doing to you.
Would you have any right to strike or revile or do any other evil
to your father or your master, if you had one, because you have
been struck or reviled by him, or received some other evil at
his hands?—you would not say this? And because we think
right to destroy you, do you think that you have any right to
destroy us in return, and your country as far as in you lies?
Will you, O professor of true virtue, pretend that you are justified in this? Has a philosopher like you failed to discover that
our country is more to be valued and higher and holier far than
mother or father or any ancestor, and more to be regarded in
the eyes of the gods and of men of understanding? also to be
soothed, and gently and reverently entreated when angry, even
more than a father, and either to be persuaded, or if not persuaded, to be obeyed? And when we are punished by her,
whether with imprisonment or stripes, the punishment is to be
endured in silence; and if she leads us to wounds or death in
battle, thither we follow as is right; neither may any one yield
or retreat or leave his rank, but whether in battle or in a court
of law, or in any other place, he must do what his city and his
country order him; or he must change their view of what is just:
and if he may do no violence to his father or mother, much less
may he do violence to his country.' What answer shall we make
to this, Crito? Do the laws speak truly, or do they not?

   Cr. I think that they do.

   Soc. Then the laws will say, 'Consider, Socrates, if we are
speaking truly that in your present attempt you are going to do
us an injury. For, having brought you into the world, and nurtured and educated you, and given you and every other citizen

a share in every good which we had to give, we further proclaim to any Athenian by the liberty which we allow him, that
if he does not like us when he has become of age and has seen
the ways of the city, and made our acquaintance, he may go
where he pleases and take his goods with him. None of us laws
will forbid him or interfere with him. Any one who does not like
us and the city, and who wants to emigrate to a colony or to
any other city, may go where he likes, retaining his property.
But he who has experience of the manner in which we order
justice and administer the state, and still remains, has entered
into an implied contract that he will do as we command him.
And he who disobeys us is, as we maintain, thrice wrong; first,
because in disobeying us he is disobeying his parents; secondly, because we are the authors of his education; thirdly,
because he has made an agreement with us that he will duly
obey our commands; and he neither obeys them nor convinces
us that our commands are unjust; and we do not rudely impose
them, but give him the alternative of obeying or convincing us;
—that is what we offer, and he does neither.

'These are the sort of accusations to which, as we were saying, you, Socrates, will be exposed if you accomplish your intentions; you, above all other Athenians.' Suppose now I ask,
why I rather than anybody else? they will justly retort upon me
that I above all other men have acknowledged the agreement.
'There is clear proof,' they will say, 'Socrates, that we and the
city were not displeasing to you. Of all Athenians you have
been the most constant resident in the city, which, as you never
leave, you may be supposed to love. For you never went out
of the city either to see the games, except once when you went
to the Isthmus, or to any other place unless when you were on
military service; nor did you travel as other men do. Nor had
you any curiosity to know other states or their laws: your affec-
tions did not go beyond us and our state; we were your special
favourites, and you acquiesced in our government of you; and
here in this city you begat your children, which is a proof of
your satisfaction. Moreover, you might in the course of the trial,
if you had liked, have fixed the penalty at banishment; the state
which refuses to let you go now would have let you go then.
But you pretended that you preferred death to exile, and that
you were not unwilling to die. And now you have forgotten
these fine sentiments, and pay no respect to us the laws, of
whom you are the destroyer; and are doing what only a miserable slave would do, running away and turning your back upon
the compacts and agreements which you made as a citizen.
And first of all answer this very question: Are we right in saying

that you agreed to be governed according to us in deed, and not in word only? Is that true or not?' How shall we answer, Crito? Must we not assent?

Cr. We cannot help it, Socrates.

Soc. Then will they not say: 'You, Socrates, are breaking the covenants and agreements which you made with us at your leisure, not in any haste or under any compulsion or deception, but after you have had seventy years to think of them, during which time you were at liberty to leave the city, if we were not to your mind, or if our covenants appeared to you to be unfair. You had your choice, and might have gone either to Lacedaemon or Crete, both which states are often praised by you for their good governments, or to some other Hellenic or foreign state. Whereas you, above all other Athenians, seemed to be so fond of the state, or, in other words, of us her laws (and who would care about a state which has no laws?), that you never stirred out of her; the halt, the blind, the maimed were not more stationary in her than you were. And now you run away and forsake your agreements. Not so, Socrates, if you will take our advice; do not make yourself ridiculous by escaping out of the city.

'For just consider, if you transgress and err in this sort of way, what good will you do either to yourself or to your friends? That your friends will be driven into exile and deprived of citizenship, or will lose their property, is tolerably certain; and you yourself, if you fly to one of the neighbouring cities, as, for example, Thebes or Megara, both of which are well governed, will come to them as an enemy, Socrates, and their government will be against you, and all patriotic citizens will cast an evil eye upon you as a subverter of the laws, and you will confirm in the minds of the judges the justice of their own condemnation of you. For he who is a corrupter of the laws is more than likely to be a corrupter of the young and foolish portion of mankind. Will you then flee from well-ordered cities and virtuous men? and is existence worth having on these terms? Or will you go to them without shame, and talk to them, Socrates? And what will you say to them? What you say here about virtue and justice and institutions and laws being the best things among men? Would that be decent of you? Surely not. But if you go away from well-governed states to Crito's friends in Thessaly, where there is great disorder and licence, they will be charmed to hear the tale of your escape from prison, set off with ludicrous particulars of the manner in which you were wrapped in a goatskin or some other disguise, and metamorphosed as the manner is of runaways; but will there be no one to remind you that in your old age you were not ashamed to violate the most sacred laws from a miserable desire of a little more life? Perhaps not, if you keep them in a good temper; but if they are out of temper you will hear many degrading things; you will live, but how?—as the flatterer of all men, and the servant of all men; and doing what?—eating and drinking in Thessaly, having gone abroad in order that you may get a dinner. And where will be your fine sentiments about justice and virtue? Say that you wish to live for the sake of your children—you want to bring them up and educate them—will you take them into Thessaly and deprive them of Athenian citizenship? Or are you under the impression that they will be better cared for and educated here if you are still alive, although absent from them; for your friends will take care of them? Do you fancy that if you are an inhabitant of Thessaly they will take care of them, and if you are an inhabitant of the other world that they will take care of them? Nay; but if they who call themselves friends are good for anything, they will—to be sure they will.

'Listen, then, Socrates, to us who have brought you up. Think not of life and children first, and of justice afterwards, but of justice first, that you may be justified before the princes of the world below. For neither will you nor any that belong to you be happier or holier or juster in this life, or happier in another, if you do as Crito bids. Now you depart in innocence, a sufferer and not a doer of evil; a victim, not of the laws but of men. But if you go forth, returning evil for evil, and injury for injury, breaking the covenants and agreements which you have made with us, and wronging those whom you ought least of all to wrong, that is to say, yourself, your friends, your country, and us, we shall be angry with you while you live, and our brethren, the laws in the world below, will receive you as an enemy; for they will know that you have done your best to destroy us. Listen, then, to us and not to Crito.'

This, dear Crito, is the voice which I seem to hear murmuring in my ears, like the sound of the flute in the ears of the mystic; that voice, I say, is humming in my ears, and prevents me from hearing any other. And I know that anything more which you may say will be vain. Yet speak, if you have anything to say.

Cr. I have nothing to say, Socrates.

Soc. Leave me then, Crito, to fulfil the will of God, and to follow whither he leads.

Henry David Thoreau

On the Duty of Civil Disobedience

I heartily accept the motto,—"That government is best which governs least;" and I should like to see it acted up to more rapidly and systematically. Carried out, it finally amounts to this, which also I believe,—"That government is best which governs not at all," and when men are prepared for it, that will be the kind of government which they will have. Government is at best but an expedient; but most governments are usually, and all governments are sometimes, inexpedient. The objections which have been brought against a standing army, and they are many and weighty, and deserve to prevail, may also at last be brought against a standing government. The standing army is only an arm of the standing government. The government itself, which is only the mode which the people have chosen to execute their will, is equally liable to be abused and perverted before the people can act through it. Witness the present Mexican war, the work of comparatively a few individuals using the standing government as their tool; for, in the outset, the people would not have consented to this measure.

This American government,—what is it but a tradition, though a recent one, endeavoring to transmit itself unimpaired to posterity, but each instant losing some of its integrity? It has not the vitality and force of a single living man; for a single

The major part of this essay was delivered as a lecture in 1848 under the title "On the Relation of the Individual to the State" and was first published in 1849 under the title "Resistance to Civil Government." It has since been published under a variety of titles—the most common being "Civil Disobedience." Thoreau (1817–1862) is best known for his book *Walden,* a diary and commentary on a year spent in a hut at Walden Pond near Concord, Massachusetts. Like most writers in the American transcendentalist tradition (which includes his friend Ralph Waldo Emerson), Thoreau's thought is eloquent and polemical rather than analytic and systematic. The essay on civil disobedience was written specifically to defend his refusal to pay taxes in support of war and slavery (a refusal which cost him a night in jail) and generally to defend individual conscience against the claims of the state. Because of his actions and this essay, Thoreau has been an inspiration to all subsequent conscientious objectors and civil disobedients. Gandhi, for example, always acknowledged the influence of Thoreau on his own thought. The essay is published here in its entirety.

man can bend it to his will. It is a sort of wooden gun to the people themselves. But it is not the less necessary for this; for the people must have some complicated machinery or other, and hear its din, to satisfy that idea of government which they have. Governments show thus how successfully men can be imposed on, even impose on themselves, for their own advantage. It is excellent, we must all allow. Yet this government never of itself furthered any enterprise, but by the alacrity with which it got out of its way. *It* does not keep the country free. *It* does not settle the West. *It* does not educate. The character inherent in the American people has done all that has been accomplished; and it would have done somewhat more, if the government had not sometimes got in its way. For government is an expedient by which men would fain succeed in letting one another alone; and, as has been said, when it is most expedient, the governed are most let alone by it. Trade and commerce, if they were not made of India-rubber, would never manage to bounce over the obstacles which legislators are continually putting in their way; and, if one were to judge these men wholly by the effects of their actions and not partly by their intentions, they would deserve to be classed and punished with those mischievous persons who put obstructions on the railroads.

But, to speak practically and as a citizen, unlike those who call themselves no-government men, I ask for, not at once no government, but *at once* a better government. Let every man make known what kind of government would command his respect, and that will be one step toward obtaining it.

After all, the practical reason why, when the power is once in the hands of the people, a majority are permitted, and for a long period continue, to rule is not because they are most likely to be in the right, nor because this seems fairest to the minority, but because they are physically the strongest. But a government in which the majority rule in all cases cannot be based on justice, even as far as men understand it. Can there not be a government in which majorities do not virtually decide right and wrong, but conscience?—in which majorities decide only those questions to which the rule of expediency is applicable? Must the citizen ever for a moment, or in the least degree, resign his conscience to the legislator? Why has every man a conscience, then? I think that we should be men first, and subjects afterward. It is not desirable to cultivate a respect for the law, so much as for the right. The only obligation which I have a right to assume is to do at any time what I think right. It is truly enough said, that a corporation has no conscience; but

a corporation of conscientious men is a corporation *with* a conscience. Law never made men a whit more just; and, by means
of their respect for it, even the well-disposed are daily made
the agents of injustice. A common and natural result of an undue respect for law is, that you may see a file of soldiers,
colonel, captain, corporal, privates, powder-monkeys, and all,
marching in admirable order over hill and dale to the wars,
against their wills, ay, against their common sense and consciences, which makes it very steep marching indeed, and
produces a palpitation of the heart. They have no doubt that
it is a damnable business in which they are concerned; they are
all peaceably inclined. Now, what are they? Men at all? or
small movable forts and magazines, at the service of some un-
scrupulous man in power? Visit the Navy-Yard, and behold a
marine, such a man as an American government can make, or
such as it can make a man with its black arts,—a mere shadow
and reminiscence of humanity, a man laid out alive and standing, and already, as one may say, buried under arms with
funeral accompaniments, though it may be,—

> Not a drum was heard, not a funeral note,
> As his corse to the rampart we hurried;
> Not a soldier discharged his farewell shot
> O'er the grave where our hero we buried.

The mass of men serve the state thus, not as men mainly,
but as machines, with their bodies. They are the standing army,
and the militia, jailors, constables, posse comitatus, etc. In
most cases there is no free exercise whatever of the judgment
or of the moral sense; but they put themselves on a level with
wood and earth and stones; and wooden men can perhaps be
manufactured that will serve the purpose as well. Such command no more respect than men of straw or a lump of dirt.
They have the same sort of worth only as horses and dogs. Yet
such as these even are commonly esteemed good citizens.
Others—as most legislators, politicians, lawyers, ministers, and
office-holders—serve the state chiefly with their heads; and, as
they rarely make any moral distinctions, they are as likely to
serve the Devil, without *intending* it, as God. A very few, as
heroes, patriots, martyrs, reformers in the great sense, and
men, serve the state with their consciences also, and so necessarily resist it for the most part; and they are commonly treated
as enemies by it. A wise man will only be useful as a man, and
will not submit to be "clay," and "stop a hole to keep the wind
away," but leave that office to his dust at least:—

I am too high-born to be propertied,
To be a secondary at control,
Or useful serving-man and instrument
To any sovereign state throughout the world.

He who gives himself entirely to his fellow-men appears to them useless and selfish; but he who gives himself partially to them is pronounced a benefactor and philanthropist.

How does it become a man to behave toward this American government to-day? I answer, that he cannot without disgrace be associated with it. I cannot for an instant recognize that political organization as *my* government which is the *slave's* government also.

All men recognize the right of revolution; that is, the right to refuse allegiance to, and to resist, the government, when its tyranny or its inefficiency are great and unendurable. But almost all say that such is not the case now. But such was the case, they think, in the Revolution of '75. If one were to tell me that this was a bad government because it taxed certain foreign commodities brought to its ports, it is most probable that I should not make an ado about it, for I can do without them. All machines have their friction; and possibly this does enough good to counterbalance the evil. At any rate, it is a great evil to make a stir about it. But when the friction comes to have its machine, and oppression and robbery are organized, I say, let us not have such a machine any longer. In other words, when a sixth of the population of a nation which has undertaken to be the refuge of liberty are slaves, and a whole country is unjustly overrun and conquered by a foreign army, and subjected to military law, I think that it is not too soon for honest men to rebel and revolutionize. What makes this duty the more urgent is the fact that the country so overrun is not our own, but ours is the invading army.

Paley,[1] a common authority with many on moral questions, in his chapter on the "Duty of Submission to Civil Government," resolves all civil obligation into expediency; and he proceeds to say, "that so long as the interest of the whole society requires it, that is, so long as the established government cannot be resisted or changed without public inconveniency, it is the will of God that the established government be obeyed, and no longer. . . . This principle being admitted, the justice

[1] [William Paley (1743–1805) had included a chapter entitled "Of the Duty of Civil Obedience, as Stated in the Christian Scriptures" in his *The Principles of Moral and Political Philosophy,* Ed.]

of every particular case of resistance is reduced to a computation of the quantity of the danger and grievance on the one side, and of the probability and expense of redressing it on the other." Of this, he says, every man shall judge for himself. But Paley appears never to have contemplated those cases to which the rule of expediency does not apply, in which a people, as well as an individual, must do justice, cost what it may. If I have unjustly wrested a plank from a drowning man, I must restore it to him though I drown myself. This, according to Paley, would be inconvenient. But he that would save his life, in such a case, shall lose it. This people must cease to hold slaves, and to make war on Mexico, though it cost them their existence as a people.

In their practice, nations agree with Paley; but does any one think that Massachusetts does exactly what is right at the present crisis?

> *A drab of state, a cloth-o'-silver slut,*
> *To have her train borne up, and her soul trail in the dirt.*

Practically speaking, the opponents to a reform in Massachusetts are not a hundred thousand politicians at the South, but a hundred thousand merchants and farmers here, who are more interested in commerce and agriculture than they are in humanity, and are not prepared to do justice to the slave and to Mexico, *cost what it may.* I quarrel not with far-off foes, but with those who, near at home, coöperate with, and do the bidding of, those far away, and without whom the latter would be harmless. We are accustomed to say, that the mass of men are unprepared; but improvement is slow, because the few are not materially wiser or better than the many. It is not so important that many should be as good as you, as that there be some absolute goodness somewhere; for that will leaven the whole lump. There are thousands who are *in opinion* opposed to slavery and to the war, who yet in effect do nothing to put an end to them; who, esteeming themselves children of Washington and Franklin, sit down with their hands in their pockets, and say that they know not what to do, and do nothing; who even postpone the question of freedom to the question of free-trade, and quietly read the prices-current along with the latest advices from Mexico, after dinner, and, it may be, fall asleep over them both. What is the price-current of an honest man and patriot to-day? They hesitate, and they regret, and sometimes they petition; but they do nothing in earnest and with effect. They will wait, well disposed, for others to remedy the evil, that they may no longer have it to regret. At most, they give only a cheap vote, and a feeble countenance and Godspeed, to the right, as it goes by them. There are nine hundred and ninety-nine patrons of virtue to one virtuous man. But it is easier to deal with the real possessor of a thing than with the temporary guardian of it.

All voting is a sort of gaming, like checkers or backgammon, with a slight moral tinge to it, a playing with right and wrong, with moral questions; and betting naturally accompanies it. The character of the voters is not staked. I cast my vote, per-chance, as I think right; but I am not vitally concerned that that right should prevail. I am willing to leave it to the majority. Its obligation, therefore, never exceeds that of expediency. Even voting *for the right* is *doing* nothing for it. It is only expressing to men feebly your desire that it should prevail. A wise man will not leave the right to the mercy of chance, nor wish it to prevail through the power of the majority. There is but little virtue in the action of masses of men. When the majority shall at length vote for the abolition of slavery, it will be because they are indifferent to slavery, or because there is but little slavery left to be abolished by their vote. *They* will then be the only slaves. Only *his* vote can hasten the abolition of slavery who asserts his own freedom by his vote.

I hear of a convention to be held at Baltimore, or elsewhere, for the selection of a candidate for the Presidency, made up chiefly of editors, and men who are politicians by profession; but I think, what is it to any independent, intelligent, and re-spectable man what decision they may come to? Shall we not have the advantage of his wisdom and honesty, nevertheless? Can we not count upon some independent votes? Are there not many individuals in the country who do not attend conventions? But no: I find that the respectable man, so called, has immedi-ately drifted from his position, and despairs of his country, when his country has more reason to despair of him. He forth-with adopts one of the candidates thus selected as the only *available* one, thus proving that he is himself *available* for any purposes of the demagogue. His vote is of no more worth than that of any unprincipled foreigner or hireling native, who may have been bought. O for a man who is a *man,* and, as my neigh-bor says, has a bone in his back which you cannot pass your hand through! Our statistics are at fault: the population has been returned too large. How many *men* are there to a square thousand miles in this country? Hardly one. Does not America offer any inducement for men to settle here? The American has dwindled into an Odd Fellow,—one who may be known by the development of his organ of gregariousness, and a manifest lack of intellect and cheerful self-reliance; whose first and chief concern, on coming into the world, is to see that the Alms-houses are in good repair; and, before yet he has lawfully donned the virile garb, to collect a fund for the support of the widows and orphans that may be; who, in short, ventures to live only by the aid of the Mutual Insurance company, which has promised to bury him decently.

It is not a man's duty, as a matter of course, to devote himself to the eradication of any, even the most enormous wrong; he may still properly have other concerns to engage him; but it is his duty, at least, to wash his hands of it, and, if he gives it no thought longer, not to give it practically his support. If I devote myself to other pursuits and contemplations, I must first see, at least, that I do not pursue them sitting upon another man's shoulders. I must get off him first, that he may pursue his con-templations too. See what gross inconsistency is tolerated. I have heard some of my townsmen say, "I should like to have them order me out to help put down an insurrection of the slaves, or to march to Mexico;—see if I would go;" and yet these very men have each, directly by their allegiance, and so indirectly, at least, by their money, furnished a substitute. The soldier is applauded who refuses to serve in an unjust war by those who do not refuse to sustain the unjust government which makes the war; is applauded by those whose own act and authority he disregards and sets at naught; as if the state were penitent to that degree that it hired one to scourge it while it sinned, but not to that degree that it left off sinning for a moment. Thus, under the name of Order and Civil Govern-ment, we are all made at last to pay homage to and support our own meanness. After the first blush of sin comes its indif-ference; and from immoral it becomes, as it were, *un*moral, and not quite unnecessary to that life which we have made.

The broadest and most prevalent error requires the most disinterested virtue to sustain it. The slight reproach to which the virtue of patriotism is commonly liable, the noble are most likely to incur. Those who, while they disapprove of the charac-ter and measures of a government, yield to it their allegiance and support are undoubtedly its most conscientious support-ers, and so frequently the most serious obstacles to reform. Some are petitioning the state to dissolve the Union, to disre-gard the requisitions of the President. Why do they not dissolve it themselves,—the union between themselves and the state,—and refuse to pay their quota into its treasury? Do not they stand in the same relation to the state that the state does to the

Union? And have not the same reasons prevented the state from resisting the Union which have prevented them from resisting the state?

How can a man be satisfied to entertain an opinion merely, and enjoy *it*? Is there any enjoyment in it, if his opinion is that he is aggrieved? If you are cheated out of a single dollar by your neighbor, you do not rest satisfied with knowing that you are cheated, or with saying that you are cheated, or even with petitioning him to pay you your due; but you take effectual steps at once to obtain the full amount, and see that you are never cheated again. Action from principle, the perception and the performance of right, changes things and relations; it is essentially revolutionary, and does not consist wholly with anything which was. It not only divides states and churches, it divides families; ay, it divides the *individual,* separating the diabolical in him from the divine.

Unjust laws exist; shall we be content to obey them, or shall we endeavor to amend them, and obey them until we have succeeded, or shall we transgress them at once? Men generally, under such a government as this, think that they ought to wait until they have persuaded the majority to alter them. They think that, if they should resist, the remedy would be worse than the evil. But it is the fault of the government itself that the remedy *is* worse than the evil. *It* makes it worse. Why is it not more apt to anticipate and provide for reform? Why does it not cherish its wise minority? Why does it cry and resist before it is hurt? Why does it not encourage its citizens to be on the alert to point out its faults and *do* better than it would have them? Why does it always crucify Christ, and excommunicate Copernicus and Luther, and pronounce Washington and Franklin rebels?

One would think, that a deliberate and practical denial of its authority was the only offense never contemplated by government; else, why has it not assigned its definite, its suitable and proportionate penalty? If a man who has no property refuses but once to earn nine shillings for the state, he is put in prison for a period unlimited by any law that I know, and determined only by the discretion of those who placed him there; but if he should steal ninety times nine shillings from the state, he is soon permitted to go at large again.

If the injustice is part of the necessary friction of the machine of government, let it go, let it go: perchance it will wear smooth, —certainly the machine will wear out. If the injustice has a spring, or a pulley, or a rope, or a crank, exclusively for itself, then perhaps you may consider whether the remedy will not be worse than the evil; but if it is of such a nature that it requires you to be the agent of injustice to another, then, I say, break the law. Let your life be a counter friction to stop the machine. What I have to do is to see, at any rate, that I do not lend myself to the wrong which I condemn.

As for adopting the ways which the state has provided for remedying the evil, I know not of such ways. They take too much time, and a man's life will be gone. I have other affairs to attend to. I came into this world, not chiefly to make this a good place to live in, but to live in it, be it good or bad. A man has not everything to do, but something; and because he cannot do *everything,* it is not necessary that he should do *something* wrong. It is not my business to be petitioning the Governor or the Legislature any more than it is theirs to petition me; and if they should not hear my petition, what should I do then? But in this case the state has provided no way: its very Constitution is the evil. This may seem to be harsh and stubborn and unconciliatory; but it is to treat with the utmost kindness and consideration the only spirit that can appreciate or deserves it. So is all change for the better, like birth and death, which convulse the body.

I do not hesitate to say, that those who call themselves Abolitionists should at once effectually withdraw their support, both in person and property, from the government of Massachusetts and not wait till they constitute a majority of one, before they suffer the right to prevail through them. I think that it is enough if they have God on their side, without waiting for that other one. Moreover, any man more right than his neighbors constitutes a majority of one already.

I meet this American government, or its representative, the state government, directly, and face to face, once a year—no more—in the person of its tax-gatherer; this is the only mode in which a man situated as I am necessarily meets it; and it then says distinctly, Recognize me; and the simplest, most effectual, and, in the present posture of affairs, the indispensablest mode of treating with it on this head, of expressing your little satisfaction with and love for it, is to deny it then. My civil neighbor, the tax-gatherer, is the very man I have to deal with, —for it is, after all, with men and not with parchment that I quarrel,—and he has voluntarily chosen to be an agent of the government. How shall he ever know well what he is and does as an officer of the government, or as a man, until he is obliged to consider whether he shall treat me, his neighbor, for whom he has respect, as a neighbor and well-disposed man, or as a maniac and disturber of the peace, and see if he can get over this obstruction to his neighborliness without a ruder and more impetuous thought or speech corresponding with his action, I know this well, that if one thousand, if one hundred, if ten men whom I could name,—if ten *honest* men only,—ay, if *one* *honest* man, in this State of Massachusetts, *ceasing to hold* *slaves,* were actually to withdraw from this copartnership, and be locked up in the county jail therefor, it would be the abolition of slavery in America. For it matters not how small the beginning may seem to be: what is once well done is done forever. But we love better to talk about it: that we say is our mission. Reform keeps many scores of newspapers in its service, but not one man. If my esteemed neighbor, the State's ambassador, who will devote his days to the settlement of the question of human rights in the Council Chamber, instead of being threatened with the prisons of Carolina, were to sit down the prisoner of Massachusetts, that State which is so anxious to foist the sin of slavery upon her sister,—though at present she can discover only an act of inhospitality to be the ground of a quarrel with her,—the Legislature would not wholly waive the subject the following winter.

Under a government which imprisons any unjustly, the true place for a just man is also a prison. The proper place to-day, the only place which Massachusetts has provided for her freer and less desponding spirits, is in her prisons, to be put out and locked out of the State by her own act, as they have already put themselves out by their principles. It is there that the fugitive slave, and the Mexican prisoner on parole, and the Indian come to plead the wrongs of his race should find them; on that separate, but more free and honorable ground, where the State places those who are not *with* her, but *against* her,—the only house in a slave State in which a free man can abide with honor. If any think that their influence would be lost there, and their voices no longer afflict the ear of the State, that they would not be as an enemy within its walls, they do not know by how much truth is stronger than error, nor how much more eloquently and effectively he can combat injustice who has experienced a little in his own person. Cast your whole vote, not a strip of paper merely, but your whole influence. A minority is powerless while it conforms to the majority; it is not even a minority then; but it is irresistible when it clogs by its whole weight. If the alternative is to keep all just men in prison, or give up war and slavery, the State will not hesitate which to choose. If a thousand men were not to pay their tax-bills this year, that would not be a violent and bloody measure, as it would be to pay them, and enable the State to commit violence and shed innocent blood. This is, in fact, the definition of a peaceable revolution, if any such is possible. If the tax-gatherer, or any other public officer, asks me, as one has done, "But what shall I do?" my answer is, "If you really wish to do anything, resign your office." When the subject has refused allegiance, and the officer has resigned his office, then the revolution is accomplished. But even suppose blood should flow. Is there not a sort of blood shed when the conscience is wounded? Through this wound a man's real manhood and immortality flow out, and he bleeds to an everlasting death. I see this blood flowing now.

I have contemplated the imprisonment of the offender, rather than the seizure of his goods,—though both will serve the same purpose,—because they who assert the purest right, and consequently are most dangerous to a corrupt State, commonly have not spent much time in accumulating property. To such the State renders comparatively small service, and a slight tax is wont to appear exorbitant, particularly if they are obliged to earn it by special labor with their hands. If there were one who lived wholly without the use of money, the State itself would hesitate to demand it of him. But the rich man—not to make any invidious comparison—is always sold to the institution which makes him rich. Absolutely speaking, the more money, the less virtue; for money comes between a man and his objects, and obtains them for him; and it was certainly no great virtue to obtain it. It puts to rest many questions which he would otherwise be taxed to answer; while the only new question which it puts is the hard but superfluous one, how to spend it. Thus his moral ground is taken from under his feet. The opportunities of living are diminished in proportion as what are called the "means" are increased. The best thing a man can do for his culture when he is rich is to endeavor to carry out those schemes which he entertained when he was poor. Christ answered the Herodians according to their condition. "Show me the tribute-money," said he;—and one took a penny out of his pocket;—if you use money which has the image of Cæsar on it and which he has made current and valuable, that is, *if you are men of the State,* and gladly enjoy the advantages of Cæsar's government, then pay him back some of his own when he demands it: "Render therefore to Cæsar that which is Cæsar's, and to God those things which are God's,"—leaving them no wiser than before as to which was which; for they did not wish to know.

When I converse with the freest of my neighbors, I perceive that, whatever they may say about the magnitude and seriousness of the question, and their regard for the public tranquillity, the long and the short of the matter is, that they cannot spare the protection of the existing government, and they dread the consequences to their property and families of disobedience to it. For my own part, I should not like to think that I ever rely on the protection of the State. But, if I deny the authority of the State when it presents its tax-bill, it will soon take and waste all my property, and so harass me and my children without end. This is hard. This makes it impossible for a man to live honestly, and at the same time comfortably, in outward respects. It will not be worth the while to accumulate property; that would be sure to go again. You must hire or squat somewhere, and raise but a small crop, and eat that soon. You must live within yourself, and depend upon yourself always tucked up and ready for a start, and not have many affairs. A man may grow rich in Turkey even, if he will be in all respects a good subject of the Turkish government. Confucius said: "If a state is governed by the principles of reason, poverty and misery are subjects of shame; if a state is not governed by the principles of reason, riches and honors are the subjects of shame." No: until I want the protection of Massachusetts to be extended to me in some distant Southern port, where my liberty is endangered, or until I am bent solely on building up an estate at home by peaceful enterprise, I can afford to refuse allegiance to Massachusetts, and her right to my property and life. It costs me less in every sense to incur the penalty of disobedience to the State than it would to obey. I should feel as if I were worth less in that case.

Some years ago, the State met me in behalf of the Church, and commanded me to pay a certain sum toward the support of a clergyman whose preaching my father attended, but never I myself. "Pay," it said, "or be locked up in the jail." I declined to pay. But, unfortunately, another man saw fit to pay it. I did not see why the schoolmaster should be taxed to support the priest, and not the priest the schoolmaster; for I was not the State's schoolmaster, but I supported myself by voluntary subscription. I did not see why the lyceum should not present its tax-bill, and have the State to back its demand, as well as the Church. However, at the request of the selectmen, I condescended to make some such statement as this in writing:—"Know all men by these presents, that I, Henry Thoreau, do not wish to be regarded as a member of any incorporated society which I have not joined." This I gave to the town clerk; and he has it. The State, having thus learned that I did not wish to be regarded as a member of that church, has never made a like demand on me since; though it said that it must adhere to its original presumption that time. If I had known how to name them, I should then have signed off in detail from all the societies which I never signed on to; but I did not know where to find a complete list.

I have paid no poll-tax for six years. I was put into a jail once on this account, for one night; and, as I stood considering the walls of solid stone, two or three feet thick, the door of wood and iron, a foot thick, and the iron grating which strained the light, I could not help being struck with the foolishness of that institution which treated me as if I were mere flesh and blood and bones, to be locked up. I wondered that it should have concluded at length that this was the best use it could put me to, and had never thought to avail itself of my services in some way. I saw that, if there was a wall of stone between me and my townsmen, there was a still more difficult one to climb or break through before they could get to be as free as I was. I did not for a moment feel confined, and the walls seemed a great waste of stone and mortar. I felt as if I alone of all my townsmen had paid my tax. They plainly did not know how to treat me, but behaved like persons who are underbred. In every threat and in every compliment there was a blunder; for they thought that my chief desire was to stand the other side of that stone wall. I could not but smile to see how industriously they locked the door on my meditations, which followed them out again without let or hindrance, and *they* were really all that was dangerous. As they could not reach me, they had resolved to punish my body; just as boys, if they cannot come at some person against whom they have a spite, will abuse his dog. I saw that the State was half-witted, that it was timid as a lone woman with her silver spoons, and that it did not know its friends from its foes, and I lost all my remaining respect for it, and pitied it.

Thus the State never intentionally confronts a man's sense, intellectual or moral, but only his body, his senses. It is not armed with superior wit or honesty, but with superior physical strength. I was not born to be forced. I will breathe after my own fashion. Let us see who is the strongest. What force has a multitude? They only can force me who obey a higher law than I. They force me to become like themselves. I do not hear of *men* being *forced* to live this way or that by masses of men. What sort of life were that to live? When I meet a government which says to me, "Your money or your life," why should I be in haste to give it my money? It may be in a great strait, and not know what to do: I cannot help that. It must help itself; do as I do. It is not worth the while to snivel about it. I am not responsible for the successful working of the machinery of society. I am not the son of the engineer. I perceive that, when an acorn and a chestnut fall side by side, the one does not remain inert to make way for the other, but both obey their own laws, and spring and grow and flourish as best they can, till one, perchance, overshadows and destroys the other. If a plant cannot live according to its nature, it dies; and so a man.

The night in prison was novel and interesting enough. The prisoners in their shirt-sleeves were enjoying a chat and the evening air in the doorway, when I entered. But the jailer said, "Come, boys, it is time to lock up;" and so they dispersed, and I heard the sound of their steps returning into the hollow apartments. My room-mate was introduced to me by the jailer as "a first-rate fellow and a clever man." When the door was locked, he showed me where to hang my hat, and how he managed matters there. The rooms were white-washed once a month; and this one, at least, was the whitest, most simply furnished, and probably the neatest apartment in the town. He naturally wanted to know where I came from, and what brought me there; and, when I had told him, I asked him in my turn how he came there, presuming him to be an honest man, of course; and, as the world goes, I believe he was. "Why," said he, "they accuse me of burning a barn; but I never did it." As near as I could discover, he had probably gone to bed in a barn when drunk, and smoked his pipe there; and so a barn was burnt. He had the reputation of being a clever man, had been there some three months waiting for his trial to come on, and would have to wait as much longer; but he was quite domesticated and contented, since he got his board for nothing, and thought that he was well treated.

He occupied one window, and I the other; and I saw that if one stayed there long, his principal business would be to look out the window. I had soon read all the tracts that were left there, and examined where former prisoners had broken out, and where a grate had been sawed off, and heard the history of the various occupants of that room; for I found that even here there was a history and a gossip which never circulated beyond the walls of the jail. Probably this is the only house in the town where verses are composed, which are afterward printed in a circular form, but not published. I was shown quite a long list of verses which were composed by some young men who had been detected in an attempt to escape, who avenged themselves by singing them.

I pumped my fellow-prisoner as dry as I could, for fear I should never see him again; but at length he showed me which was my bed, and left me to blow out the lamp.

It was like traveling into a far country, such as I had never expected to behold, to lie there for one night. It seemed to me that I never had heard the town-clock strike before, nor the evening sounds of the village; for we slept with the windows open, which were inside the grating. It was to see my native village in the light of the Middle Ages, and our Concord was turned into a Rhine stream, and visions of knights and castles passed before me. They were the voices of old burghers that I heard in the streets. I was an involuntary spectator and auditor of whatever was done and said in the kitchen of the adjacent village-inn,—a wholly new and rare experience to me. It was a closer view of my native town. I was fairly inside of it. I never had seen its institutions before. This is one of its peculiar institutions; for it is a shire town. I began to comprehend what its inhabitants were about.

In the morning, our breakfasts were put through the hole in the door, in small oblong-square tin pans, made to fit, and holding a pint of chocolate, with brown bread, and an iron spoon. When they called for the vessels again, I was green enough to return what bread I had left; but my comrade seized it, and said that I should lay that up for lunch or dinner. Soon after he was let out to work at haying in a neighboring field, whither he went every day, and would not be back till noon; so he bade me good-day, saying that he doubted if he should see me again.

When I came out of prison,—for some one interfered, and paid that tax,—I did not perceive that great changes had taken place on the common, such as he observed who went in a youth and emerged a tottering and gray-headed man; and yet a change had to my eyes come over the scene,—the town, and State, and country,—greater than any that mere time could effect. I saw yet more distinctly the State in which I lived. I saw to what extent the people among whom I lived could be trusted as good neighbors and friends; that their friendship was for summer weather only; that they did not greatly propose to do right; that they were a distinct race from me by their prejudices and superstitions, as the Chinamen and Malays are; that in their sacrifices to humanity they ran no risks, not even to their property; that after all they were not so noble but they treated the thief as he had treated them, and hoped, by a certain outward observance and a few prayers, and by walking in a particular straight though useless path from time to time, to save their souls. This may be to judge my neighbors harshly; for I believe that many of them are not aware that they have such an institution as the jail in their village.

It was formerly the custom in our village, when a poor debtor came out of jail, for his acquaintances to salute him, looking through their fingers, which were crossed to represent the grating of a jail window, "How do ye do?" My neighbors did not thus salute me, but first looked at me, and then at one another, as if I had returned from a long journey. I was put into jail as I was going to the shoemaker's to get a shoe which was mended. When I was let out the next morning, I proceeded to finish my errand, and, having put on my mended shoe, joined a huckleberry party, who were impatient to put themselves under my conduct; and in half an hour,—for the horse was soon tackled,—was in the midst of a huckleberry field, on one of our highest hills, two miles off, and then the State was nowhere to be seen.

This is the whole history of "My Prisons."

I have never declined paying the highway tax, because I am as desirous of being a good neighbor as I am of being a bad subject; and as for supporting schools, I am doing my part to educate my fellow-countrymen now. It is for no particular item in the tax-bill that I refuse to pay it. I simply wish to refuse allegiance to the State, to withdraw and stand aloof from it effectually. I do not care to trace the course of my dollar, if I could, till it buys a man or musket to shoot with,—the dollar is innocent,—but I am concerned to trace the effects of my allegiance. In fact, I quietly declare war with the State, after my fashion, though I will still make what use and get what advantage of her I can, as is usual in such cases.

If others pay the tax which is demanded of me, from a sympathy with the State, they do but what they have already done in their own case, or rather they abet injustice to a greater extent than the State requires. If they pay the tax from a mistaken interest in the individual taxed, to save his property, or prevent his going to jail, it is because they have not considered wisely how far they let their private feelings interfere with the public good.

This, then, is my position at present. But one cannot be too much on his guard in such a case, lest his action be biased by obstinacy or an undue regard for the opinions of men. Let him see that he does only what belongs to himself and to the hour.

I think sometimes, Why, this people mean well, they are only ignorant; they would do better if they knew how: why give your neighbors this pain to treat you as they are not inclined to? But I think again, This is no reason why I should do as they do, or permit others to suffer much greater pain of a different kind. Again, I sometimes say to myself, When many millions of men, without heat, without ill will, without personal feeling of any kind, demand of you a few shillings only, without the possibility, such is their constitution, of retracting or altering their present demand, and without the possibility, on your side, of appeal to any other millions, why expose yourself to this overwhelming brute force? You do not resist cold and hunger, the winds and the waves, thus obstinately; you quietly submit to a thousand similar necessities. You do not put your head into the fire. But just in proportion as I regard this as not wholly a brute force, but partly a human force, and consider that I have relations to those millions as to so many millions of men, and not of mere brute or inanimate things, I see that appeal is possible, first and instantaneously, from them to the Maker of them, and, secondly, from them to themselves. But if I put my head deliberately into the fire, there is no appeal to fire or to the Maker of fire, and I have only myself to blame. If I could convince myself that I have any right to be satisfied with men as they are, and to treat them accordingly, and not according, in some respects, to my requisitions and expectations of what they and I ought to be, then, like a good Mussulman and fatalist, I should endeavor to be satisfied with things as they are, and say it is the will of God. And, above all, there is this difference between resisting this and a purely brute or natural force, that I can resist this with some effect; but I cannot expect, like Orpheus, to change the nature of the rocks and trees and beasts.

I do not wish to quarrel with any man or nation. I do not wish to split hairs, to make fine distinctions, or set myself up as better than my neighbors. I seek rather, I may say, even an excuse for conforming to the laws of the land. I am but too ready to conform to them. Indeed, I have reason to suspect myself on this head; and each year, as the tax-gatherer comes round, I find myself disposed to review the acts and position of the general and State governments, and the spirit of the people, to discover a pretext for conformity.

> We must affect our country as our parents,
> And if at any time we alienate
> Our love or industry from doing it honor,
> We must respect effects and teach the soul
> Matter of conscience and religion,
> And not desire of rule or benefit.

I believe that the State will soon be able to take all my work of this sort out of my hands, and then I shall be no better a patriot than my fellow-countrymen. Seen from a lower point of view, the Constitution, with all its faults, is very good; the law and the courts are very respectable; even this State and this American government are, in many respects, very admirable, and rare things, to be thankful for, such as a great many have described them; but seen from a point of view a little higher, they are what I have described them; seen from a higher still, and the highest, who shall say what they are, or that they are worth looking at or thinking of at all?

However, the government does not concern me much, and I shall bestow the fewest possible thoughts on it. It is not many moments that I live under a government, even in this world. If a man is thought-free, fancy-free, imagination-free, that which *is not* never for a long time appearing *to be* to him, unwise rulers or reformers cannot fatally interrupt him.

I know that most men think differently from myself; but those whose lives are by profession devoted to the study of these or kindred subjects content me as little as any. Statesmen and legislators, standing so completely within the institution, never distinctly and nakedly behold it. They speak of moving society, but have no resting-place without it. They may be men of a certain experience and discrimination, and have no doubt invented ingenious and even useful systems, for which we sincerely thank them; but all their wit and usefulness lie within certain not very wide limits. They are wont to forget that the world is not governed by policy and expediency. Webster never goes behind government, and so cannot speak with authority about it. His words are wisdom to those legislators who contemplate no essential reform in the existing government; but for thinkers, and those who legislate for all time, he never once glances at the subject. I know of those whose serene and wise speculations on this theme would soon reveal the limits of his mind's range and hospitality. Yet, compared with the cheap professions of most reformers, and the still cheaper wisdom and eloquence of politicians in general, his are almost the only sensible and valuable words, and we thank Heaven for him. Comparatively, he is always strong, original, and, above all, practical. Still, his quality is not wisdom, but prudence. The lawyer's truth is not Truth, but consistency or a consistent expediency. Trust is always in harmony with herself, and is not concerned chiefly to reveal the justice that may consist with wrong-doing. He well deserves to be called, as he has been called, the Defender of the Constitution. There are really no blows to be given by him but defensive ones. He is not a leader, but a follower. His leaders are the men of '87. "I have never made an effort," he says, "and never propose to make an effort; I have never countenanced an effort, and never mean to countenance an effort, to disturb the arrangement as originally made, by which the various States came into the Union." Still thinking of the sanction which the Constitution gives to slavery, he says, "Because it was a part of the original compact,—let it stand." Notwithstanding his special acuteness and ability, he is unable to take a fact out of its merely political relations, and behold it as it lies absolutely to be disposed of by the intellect, —what, for instance, it behooves a man to do here in America to-day with regard to slavery,—but ventures, or is driven, to make some such desperate answer as the following, while professing to speak absolutely, and as a private man,—from which what new and singular code of social duties might be inferred? "The manner," says he, "in which the governments of those States where slavery exists are to regulate it is for their own consideration, under their responsibility to their constituents, to the general laws of propriety, humanity, and justice, and to God. Associations formed elsewere, springing from a feeling of humanity, or other cause, have nothing whatever to do with it. They have never received any encouragement from me, and they never will."

They who know of no purer sources of truth, who have traced up its stream no higher, stand, and wisely stand, by the Bible and the Constitution, and drink at it there with reverence and humility; but they who behold where it comes trickling into this lake or that pool, gird up their loins once more, and continue their pilgrimage toward its fountainhead.

No man with a genius for legislation has appeared in America. They are rare in the history of the world. There are orators, politicians, and eloquent men, by the thousand; but the speaker has not yet opened his mouth to speak who is capable of settling the much-vexed questions of the day. We love eloquence for its own sake, and not for any truth which it may utter, or any heroism it may inspire. Our legislators have not yet learned the comparative value of free-trade and of freedom, of union, and of rectitude, to a nation. They have no genius or talent for comparatively humble questions of taxation and finance, commerce and manufactures and agriculture. If we were left solely to the wordy wit of legislators in Congress for our guidance, uncorrected by the seasonable experience and the effectual complaints of the people, America would not long retain her rank among the nations. For eighteen hundred years, though perchance I have no right to say it, the New Testament has been written; yet where is the legislator who has wisdom and practical talent enough to avail himself of the light which it sheds on the science of legislation?

The authority of government, even such as I am willing to submit to,—for I will cheerfully obey those who know and can do better than I, and in many things even those who neither know nor can do so well,—is still an impure one: to be strictly just, it must have the sanction and consent of the governed. It can have no pure right over my person and property but what I concede to it. The progress from an absolute to a limited monarchy, from a limited monarchy to a democracy, is a progress toward a true respect for the individual. Even the Chinese philosopher was wise enough to regard the individual as the basis of the empire. Is a democracy, such as we know it, the last improvement possible in government? Is it not possible to take a step further towards recognizing and organizing the rights of man? There will never be a really free and enlightened State until the State comes to recognize the individual as a higher and independent power, from which all its own power and authority are derived, and treats him accordingly. I please myself with imagining a State at last which can afford to be just to all men, and to treat the individual with respect as a neighbor; which even would not think it inconsistent with its own repose if a few were to live aloof from it, not meddling with it, nor embraced by it, who fulfilled all the duties of neighbors and fellowmen. A State which bore this kind of fruit, and suffered it to drop off as fast as it ripened, would prepare the way for a still more perfect and glorious State, which also I have imagined, but not yet anywhere seen.

John Rawls

Legal Obligation and the Duty of Fair Play

1. The subject of law and morality suggests many different questions. In particular, it may consider the historical and sociological question as to the way and manner in which moral ideas influence and are influenced by the legal system; or it may involve the question whether moral concepts and principles enter into an adequate definition of law. Again, the topic of law and morality suggests the problem of the legal enforcement of morality and whether the fact that certain conduct is immoral by accepted precepts is sufficient to justify making that conduct a legal offense. Finally, there is the large subject of the study of the rational principles of moral criticism of legal institutions and the moral grounds of our acquiescence in them. I shall be concerned solely with a fragment of this last question: with the grounds for our moral obligation to obey the law, that is, to carry out our legal duties and to fulfill our legal obligations. My thesis is that the moral obligation to obey the law is a special case of the prima facie duty of fair play.

I shall assume, as requiring no argument, that there is, at least in a society such as ours, a moral obligation to obey the law, although it may, of course, be overridden in certain cases by other more stringent obligations. I shall assume also that this obligation must rest on some general moral principle; that is, it must depend on some principle of justice or upon some principle of social utility or the common good, and the like. Now, it may appear to be a truism, and let us suppose it is, that

Reprinted by permission of New York University Press from *Law and Philosophy* by Sidney Hook, © 1964 by New York University. John Rawls is a Professor of Philosophy at Harvard University and is the author of several extemely influential articles in moral and political philosophy: "Two Concepts of Rules," 1955; "Outline of a Decision Procedure for Ethics," 1957; "Justice as Fairness," 1958; "The Sense of Justice," 1963—all in *The Philosophical Review;* "Constitutional Liberty and the Concept of Justice," *Nomos VI: Justice,* ed. Carl J. Friedrich and John W. Chapman (New York, 1963); and "Distributive Justice," *Philosophy, Politics, and Society,* Third Series, ed. Peter Laslett and W. G. Runciman (Oxford, 1967). He has further explored the topics of obligation to obey the law and civil disobedience in his "The Justification of Civil Disobedience," *Civil Disobedience: Theory and Practice,* ed. Hugo Adam Bedau (New York, 1969).

a moral obligation rests on some moral principle. But I mean to exclude the possibility that the obligation to obey the law is based on a special principle of its own. After all, it is not, without further argument, absurd that there is a moral principle such that when we find ourselves subject to an existing system of rules satisfying the definition of a legal system, we have an obligation to obey the law; and such a principle might be final, and not in need of explanation, in the way in which the principles of justice or of promising and the like are final. I do not know of anyone who has said that there is a special principle of legal obligation in this sense. Given a rough agreement, say, on the possible principles as being those of justice, of social utility, and the like, the question has been on which of one or several is the obligation to obey the law founded, and which, if any, has a special importance. I want to give a special place to the principle defining the duty of fair play.

2. In speaking of one's obligation to obey the law, I am using the term "obligation" in its more limited sense, in which, together with the notion of a duty and of a responsibility, it has a connection with institutional rules. Duties and responsibilities are assigned to certain positions and offices, and obligations are normally the consequence of voluntary acts of persons, and while perhaps most of our obligations are assumed by ourselves, through the making of promises and the accepting of benefits, and so forth, others may put us under obligation to them (as when on some occasion they help us, for example, as children). I should not claim that the moral grounds for our obeying the law is derived from the duty of fair-play except insofar as one is referring to an obligation in this sense. It would be incorrect to say that our duty not to commit any of the legal offenses, specifying crimes of violence, is based on the duty of fair play, at least entirely. These crimes involve wrongs as such, and with such offenses, as with the vices of cruelty and greed, our doing them is wrong independently of there being a legal system the benefits of which we have voluntarily accepted.

I shall assume several special features about the nature of the legal order in regard to which a moral obligation arises. In addition to the generally strategic place of its system of rules, as defining and relating the fundamental institutions of society that regulate the pursuit of substantive interests, and to the monopoly of coercive powers, I shall suppose that the legal system in question satisfies the concept of the *rule of law* (or what one may think of as justice as regularity). By this I mean that its rules are public, that similar cases are treated similarly, that there are no bills of attainder, and the like. These are all features of a legal system insofar as it embodies without deviation the notion of a public system of rules addressed to rational beings for the organization of their conduct in the pursuit of their substantive interests. This concept imposes, by itself, no limits on the *content* of legal rules, but only on their regular administration. Finally, I shall assume that the legal order is that of a constitutional democracy: that is, I shall suppose that there is a constitution establishing a position of equal citizenship and securing freedom of the person, freedom of thought and liberty of conscience, and such political equality as in suffrage and the right to participate in the political process. Thus I am confining discussion to a legal system of a special kind, but there is no harm in this.

3. The moral grounds of legal obligation may be brought out by considering what at first seem to be two anomalous facts: first, that sometimes we have an obligation to obey what we think, and think correctly, is an unjust law; and second, that sometimes we have an obligation to obey a law even in a situation where more good (thought of as a sum of social advantages) would seem to result from not doing so. If the moral obligation to obey the law is founded on the principle of fair play, how can one become bound to obey an unjust law, and what is there about the principle that explains the grounds for forgoing the greater good?

It is, of course, a familiar situation in a constitutional democracy that a person finds himself morally obligated to obey an unjust law. This will be the case whenever a member of the minority, on some legislative proposal, opposes the majority view for reasons of justice. Perhaps the standard case is where the majority, or a coalition sufficient to constitute a majority, takes advantage of its strength and votes in its own interests. But this feature is not essential. A person belonging to the minority may be advantaged by the majority proposal and still oppose it as unjust, yet when it is enacted he will normally be bound by it.

Some have thought that there is ostensibly a paradox of a special kind when a citizen, who votes in accordance with his moral principles (conception of justice), accepts the majority decision when he is in the minority. Let us suppose the vote is between two bills, *A* and *B* each establishing an income tax procedure, rates of progression, or the like, which are contrary to one another. Suppose further that one thinks of the constitutional procedure for enacting legislation as a sort of machine that yields a result when the votes are fed into it—the result being that a certain bill is enacted. The question arises as to how a citizen can accept the machine's choice, which (assuming that B gets a majority of the votes) involves thinking that B ought to be enacted when, let us suppose, he is of the declared opinion that A ought to be enacted. For some the paradox seems to be that in a constitutional democracy a citizen is often put in a situation of believing that both A and B should be enacted when A and B are contraries: that A should be enacted because A is the best policy, and that B should be enacted because B has a majority—and moreover, and this is essential, that this conflict is different from the usual sort of conflict between prima facie duties.

There are a number of things that may be said about this supposed paradox, and there are several ways in which it may be resolved, each of which brings out an aspect of the situation. But I think the simplest thing to say is to deny straightaway that there is anything different in this situation than in any other situation where there is a conflict of prima facie principles. The essential of the matter seems to be as follows: (1) Should A or B be enacted and implemented, that is, administered? Since it is supposed that everyone accepts the outcome of the vote, within limits, it is appropriate to put the enactment and implementation together. (2) Is A or B the best policy? It is assumed that everyone votes according to his political opinion as to which is the best policy and that the decision as to how to vote is not based on personal interest. There is no special conflict in this situation: the citizen who knows that he will find himself in the minority believes that, taking into account only the relative merits of A and B as prospective statutes, and leaving aside how the vote will go, A should be enacted and implemented. Moreover, on his own principles he should vote for what he thinks is the best policy, and leave aside how the vote will go. On the other hand, given that a majority will vote for B, B should be enacted and implemented, and he may know that a majority will vote for B. These judgments are relative to different principles (different arguments). The first is based on the person's conception of the best social policy; the second is based on the principles on which he accepts the constitution. The real decision, then, is as follows: A person has to decide, in each case where he is in the minority, whether the nature of the statute is such that, given that it will get, or has got, a majority vote, he should oppose its being implemented, engage in civil disobedience, or take equivalent action. In this situation he simply has to balance his obligation to oppose an unjust statute against his obligation to abide by a just constitution. This is, of course, a difficult situation, but not one introducing any deep logical paradox. Normally, it is hoped that the obligation to the constitution is clearly the decisive one.

Although it is obvious, it may be worthwhile mentioning, since a relevant feature of voting will be brought out, that the result of a vote is that a rule of law is enacted, and although given the fact of its enactment, everyone agrees that it should be implemented, no one is required to believe that the statute enacted represents the best policy. It is consistent to say that another statute would have been better. The vote does not result in a statement to be believed: namely, that *B* is superior, on its merits, to *A*. To get this interpretation one would have to suppose that the principles of the constitution specify a device which gathers information as to what citizens think should be done and that the device is so constructed that it always produces from this information the morally correct opinion as to which is the best policy. If in accepting a constitution it was so interpreted, there would, indeed, be a serious paradox: for a citizen would be torn between believing, on his own principles, that *A* is the best policy, and believing at the same time that *B* is the best policy as established by the constitutional device, the principles of the design of which he accepts. This conflict could be made a normal one only if one supposed that a person who made his own judgment on the merits was always prepared to revise it given the opinion constructed by the machine. But it is not possible to determine the best policy in this way, nor is it possible for a person to give such an undertaking. What this misinterpretation of the constitutional procedure shows, I think, is that there is an important difference between voting and spending. The constitutional procedure is not, in an essential respect, the same as the market: Given the usual assumptions of perfect competition of price theory, the actions of private persons spending according to their interests will result in the best situation, as judged by the criterion of Pareto. But in a perfectly just constitutional procedure, people voting their political opinions on the merits of policies may or may not reflect the best policy. What this misinterpretation brings out, then, is that when citizens vote for policies on their merits, the constitutional procedure cannot be viewed as acting as the market does, even under ideal conditions. A constitutional procedure does not reconcile differences of opinion into an opinion to be taken as true—this can only be done by argument and reasoning—but rather it decides whose opinion is to determine legislative policy.

4. Now to turn to the main problem, that of understanding how a person can properly find himself in a position where, by his own principles, he must grant that, given a majority vote, *B* should be enacted and implemented even though *B* is unjust. There is, then, the question as to how it can be morally justifiable to acknowledge a constitutional procedure for making legislative enactments when it is certain (for all practical purposes) that laws will be passed that by one's own principles are unjust. It would be impossible for a person to undertake to change his mind whenever he found himself in the minority; it is not impossible, but entirely reasonable, for him to undertake to abide by the enactments made, whatever they are, provided that they are within certain limits. But what more exactly are the conditions of this undertaking?

First of all, it means, as previously suggested, that the constitutional procedure is misinterpreted as a procedure for making legal rules. It is a process of social decision that does not produce a statement to be believed (that *B* is the best policy) but a rule to be followed. Such a procedure, say involving some form of majority rule, is necessary because it is certain that there will be disagreement on what is the best policy. This will be true even if we assume, as I shall, that everyone has a similar sense of justice and everyone is able to agree on a certain constitutional procedure as just. There will be disagreement because they will not approach issues with the same stock of information, they will regard different moral features of situations as carrying different weights, and so on. The acceptance of a constitutional procedure is, then, a necessary political device to decide between conflicting legislative proposals. If one thinks of the constitution as a fundamental part of the scheme of social cooperation, then one can say that if the constitution is just, and if one has accepted the benefits of its working and intends to continue doing so, and if the rule enacted is within certain limits, then one has an obligation, based on the principle of fair play, to obey it when it comes one's turn. In accepting the benefits of a just constitution one becomes bound to it, and in particular one becomes bound to one of its fundamental rules: given a majority vote in behalf of a statute, it is to be enacted and properly implemented.

The principle of fair play may be defined as follows. Suppose there is a mutually beneficial and just scheme of social cooperation, and that the advantages it yields can only be obtained if everyone, or nearly everyone, cooperates. Suppose further that cooperation requires a certain sacrifice from each person, or at least involves a certain restriction of his liberty. Suppose finally that the benefits produced by cooperation are, up to a certain point, free: that is, the scheme of cooperation is unstable in the sense that if any one person knows that all (or nearly all) of the others will continue to do their part, he will still be able to share a gain from the scheme even if he does not do his part. Under these conditions a person who has accepted the benefits of the scheme is bound by a duty of fair play to do his part and not to take advantage of the free benefit by not cooperating. The reason one must abstain from this attempt is that the existence of the benefit is the result of everyone's effort, and prior to some understanding as to how it is to be shared, if it can be shared at all, it belongs in fairness to no one. (I return to this question below.)

Now I want to hold that the obligation to obey the law, as enacted by a constitutional procedure, even when the law seems unjust to us, is a case of the duty of fair play as defined. It is, moreover, an obligation in the more limited sense in that it depends upon our having accepted and our intention to continue accepting the benefits of a just scheme of cooperation that the constitution defines. In this sense it depends on our own voluntary acts. Again, it is an obligation owed to our fellow citizens generally: that is, to those who cooperate with us in the working of the constitution. It is not an obligation owed to public officials, although there may be such obligations. That it is an obligation owed by citizens to one another is shown by the fact that they are entitled to be indignant with one another for failure to comply. Further, an essential condition of the obligation is the justice of the constitution and the general system of law being roughly in accordance with it. Thus the obligation to obey (or not to resist) an unjust law depends strongly on there being a just constitution. Unless one obeys the law enacted under it, the proper equilibrium, or balance, between competing claims defined by the constitution will not be maintained. Finally, while it is true enough to say that the enactment by a majority binds the minority, so that one may be bound by the acts of others, there is no question of their binding them in conscience to certain beliefs as to what is the best policy, and it is a necessary condition of the acts of others binding us that the constitution is just, that we have accepted its benefits, and so forth.

5. Now a few remarks about the principles of a just constitution. Here I shall have to presuppose a number of things about the principles of justice. In particular, I shall assume that there are two principles of justice that properly apply to the fundamental structure of institutions of the social system and,

thus, to the constitution. The first of these principles requires that everyone have an equal right to the most extensive liberty compatible with a like liberty for all; the second is that inequalities are arbitrary unless it is reasonable to expect that they will work out for everyone's advantage and provided that the positions and offices to which they attach or from which they may be gained are open to all. I shall assume that these are the principles that can be derived by imposing the constraints of morality upon rational and mutually self-interested persons when they make conflicting claims on the basic form of their common institutions: that is, when questions of justice arise.

The principle relevant at this point is the first principle, that of equal liberty. I think it may be argued with some plausibility that it requires, where it is possible, the various equal liberties in a constitutional democracy. And once these liberties are established and constitutional procedures exist, one can view legislation as rules enacted that must be ostensibly compatible with both principles. Each citizen must decide as best he can whether a piece of legislation, say the income tax, violates either principle; and this judgment depends on a wide body of social facts. Even in a society of impartial and rational persons, one cannot expect agreement on these matters.

Now recall that the question is this: How is it possible that a person, in accordance with his own conception of justice, should find himself bound by the acts of another to obey an unjust law (not simply a law contrary to his interests)? Put another way: Why, when I am free and still without my chains, should I accept certain a priori conditions to which any social contract must conform, a priori conditions that rule out all constitutional procedures that would decide in accordance with my judgment of justice against everyone else? To explain this (Little has remarked),[1] we require two hypotheses: that among the very limited number of procedures that would stand any chance of being established, none would make my decision decisive in this way; and that all such procedures would determine social conditions that I judge to be better than anarchy. Granting the second hypothesis, I want to elaborate on this in the following way: the first step in the explanation is to

---

[1] The metaphor of being free and without one's chains is taken from I. M. D. Little's review of K. Arrow's book *Social Choice and Individual Values* (New York, 1951), which appeared in *Journal of Political Economy*, LX (1952). See p. 431. My argument follows his in all essential respects, the only addition being that I have introduced the concept of justice in accounting for what is, in effect, Arrow's non-dictatorship condition.

derive the principles of justice that are to apply to the basic form of the social system and, in particular, to the constitution. Once we have these principles, we see that no just constitutional procedure would make my judgment as to the best policy decisive (would make me a dictator in Arrow's sense).[2] It is not simply that, among the limited number of procedures actually possible as things are, no procedure would give me this authority. The point is that even if such were possible, given some extraordinary social circumstances, it would not be just. (Of course it is not possible for everyone to have this authority.) Once we see this, we see how it is possible that within the framework of a just constitutional procedure to which we are obligated, it may nevertheless happen that we are bound to obey what seems to us to be and is an unjust law. Moreover, the possibility is present even though everyone has the same sense of justice (that is, accepts the same principles of justice) and everyone regards the constitutional procedure itself as just. Even the most efficient constitution cannot prevent the enactment of unjust laws if, from the complexity of the social situation and like conditions, the majority decides to enact them. A just constitutional procedure cannot foreclose all injustice; this depends on those who carry out the procedure. A constitutional procedure is not like a market reconciling interests to an optimum result.

6. So far I have been discussing the first mentioned anomaly of legal obligation, namely, that though it is founded on justice, we may be required to obey an unjust law. I should now like to include the second anomaly: that we may have an obligation to obey the law even though more good (thought of as a sum of advantages) may be gained by not doing so. The thesis I wish to argue is that not only is our obligation to obey the law a special case of the principle of fair play, and so dependent upon the justice of the institutions to which we are obligated, but also the principles of justice are absolute with respect to the principle of utility (as the principle to maximize the net sum of advantages). By this I mean two things. First, unjust institutions cannot be justified by an appeal to the principle of utility. A greater balance of net advantages shared by some cannot justify the injustice suffered by others; and where unjust institutions are tolerable it is because a certain degree of injustice sometimes cannot be avoided, that social necessity requires it, that there would be greater injustice otherwise, and so on. Second, our obligation to obey the law, which is a

[2] See Arrow, *opus cit. supra.*

special case of the principle of fair play, cannot be overridden by an appeal to utility, though it may be overridden by another duty of justice. These are sweeping propositions and most likely false, but I should like to examine them briefly.

I do not know how to establish these propositions. They are not established by the sort of argument used above to show that the two principles, previously mentioned, are the two principles of justice, that is, when the subject is the basic structure of the social system. What such an argument might show is that, if certain natural conditions are taken as specifying the concept of justice, then the two principles of justice are the principles logically associated with the concept when the subject is the basic structure of the social system. The argument might prove, if it is correct, that the principles of justice are incompatible with the principle of utility. The argument might establish that our intuitive notions of justice must sometimes conflict with the principle of utility. But it leaves unsettled what the more general notion of right requires when this conflict occurs. To prove that the concept of justice should have an absolute weight with respect to that of utility would require a deeper argument based on an analysis of the concept of right, at least insofar as it relates to the concepts of justice and utility. I have no idea whether such an analysis is possible. What I propose to do instead is to try out the thought that the concept of justice does have an absolute weight, and to see whether this suggestion, in view of our considered moral opinions, leads to conclusions that we cannot accept. It would seem as if to attribute to justice an absolute weight is to interpret the concept of right as requiring that a special place be given to persons capable of a sense of justice and to the principle of their working out together, from an initial position of equality, the form of their common institutions. To the extent that this idea is attractive, the concept of justice will tend to have an absolute weight with respect to utility.

7. Now to consider the two anomalous cases. First: In the situation where the obligation requires obedience to an unjust law, it seems true to say that the obligation depends on the principle of fair play and, thus, on justice. Suppose it is a matter of a person being required to pay an income tax of a kind that he thinks is unjust, not simply by reference to his interests. He would not want to try to justify the tax on the ground that the net gain to certain groups in society is such as to outweigh the injustice. The natural argument to make is to his obligation to a just constitution.

But in considering a particular issue, a citizen has to make two decisions: how he will vote (and I assume that he votes for what he thinks is the best policy, morally speaking), and, in case he should be in the minority, whether his obligation to support, or not obstruct, the implementation of the law enacted is not overridden by a stronger obligation that may lead to a number of courses including civil disobedience. Now in the sort of case imagined, suppose there is a real question as to whether the tax law should be obeyed. Suppose, for example, that it is framed in such a way that it seems deliberately calculated to undermine unjustly the position of certain social or religious groups. Whether the law should be obeyed or not depends, if one wants to emphasize the notion of justice, on such matters as (1) the justice of the constitution and the real opportunity it allows for reversal; (2) the depth of the injustice of the law enacted; (3) whether the enactment is actually a matter of calculated intent by the majority and warns of further such acts; and (4) whether the political sociology of the situation is such as to allow of hope that the law may be repealed. Certainly, if a social or religious group reasonably (not irrationally) and correctly supposes that a permanent majority, or majority coalition, has deliberately set out to undercut its basis and that there is no chance of successful constitutional resistance, then the obligation to obey that particular law (and perhaps other laws more generally) ceases. In such a case a minority may no longer be obligated by the duty of fair play. There may be other reasons, of course, at least for a time, for obeying the law. One might say that disobedience will not improve the justice of their situation or their descendants' situation; or that it will result in injury and harm to innocent persons (that is, members not belonging to the unjust majority). In this way, one might appeal to the balance of justice, if the principle of not causing injury to the innocent is a question of justice; but in any case, the appeal is not made to the greater net balance of advantages (irrespective of the moral position of those receiving them). The thesis I want to suggest then, is that in considering whether we are obligated to obey an unjust law, one is led into no absurdity if one simply throws out the principle of utility altogether, except insofar as it is included in the general principle requiring one to establish the most efficient just institutions.

Second: Now the other sort of anomaly arises when the law is just and we have a duty of fair play to follow it, but a greater net balance of advantages could be gained from not doing so. Again the income tax will serve to illustrate this familiar point: The social consequences of any one person (perhaps even many people) not paying his tax are unnoticeable, and let us suppose zero in value, but there is a noticeable private gain for the person himself, or for another to whom he chooses to give it (the institution of the income tax is subject to the first kind of instability). The duty of fair play binds us to pay our tax, nevertheless, since we have accepted, and intend to continue doing so, the benefits of the fiscal system to which the income tax belongs. Why is this reasonable and not a blind following of a rule, when a greater net sum of advantages is possible?—because the system of cooperation consistently followed by everyone else itself produces the advantages generally enjoyed and in the case of a practice such as the income tax there is no reason to given exemptions to anyone so that they might enjoy the possible benefit. (An analogous case is the moral obligation to vote and so to work the constitutional procedure from which one has benefited. This obligation cannot be overridden by the fact that our vote never makes a difference in the outcome of an election; it may be overridden, however, by a number of other considerations, such as a person being disenchanted with all parties, being excusably uninformed, and the like.)

There are cases, on the other hand, where a certain number of exemptions can be arranged for in a just or fair way; and if so, the practice, including the exemptions, is more efficient, and when possible it should be adopted (waiving problems of transition) in accordance with the principle of establishing the most efficient just practice. For example, in the familiar instance of the regulation to conserve water in a drought, it might be ascertained that there would be no harm in a certain extra use of water over and above the use for drinking. In this case some rotation scheme can be adopted that allots exemptions in a fair way, such as houses on opposite sides of the street being given exemptions on alternate days. The details are not significant here. The main idea is simply that if the greater sum of advantages can effectively and fairly be distributed amongst those whose cooperation makes these advantages possible, then this should be done. It would indeed be irrational to prefer a lesser to a more efficient just scheme of cooperation; but this fact is not to be confused with justifying an unjust scheme by its greater efficiency or excusing ourselves from a duty of fair play by an appeal to utility. If there is no reason to distribute the possible benefit, as in the case of the income tax, or in the case of voting, or if there is no way to do so that does not involve such problems as excessive costs, then the benefit should be foregone. One may disagree with this view, but it is not irrational, not a matter of rule worship: it is, rather, an appeal to the duty of fair play, which requires one to abstain from an advantage that cannot be distributed fairly to those whose efforts have made it possible. That those who make the efforts and undergo the restrictions of their liberty should share in the benefits produced is a consequence of the assumption of an initial position of equality, and it falls under the second principle. But the question of distributive justice is too involved to go into here. Moreover, it is unlikely that there is any substantial social benefit for the distribution of which some fair arrangement cannot be made.

8. To summarize, I have suggested that the following propositions may be true:

First, that our moral obligation to obey the law is a special case of the duty of fair play. This means that the legal order is construed as a system of social cooperation to which we become bound because: first, the scheme is just (that is, it satisfies the two principles of justice), and no just scheme can ensure against our ever being in the minority in a vote; and second, we have accepted, and intend to continue to accept, its benefits. If we failed to obey the law, to act on our duty of fair play, the equilibrium between conflicting claims, as defined by the concept of justice, would be upset. The duty of fair play is not, of course, intended to account for its being wrong for us to commit crimes of violence, but it is intended to account, in part, for the obligation to pay our income tax, to vote, and so on.

Second, I then suggested that the concept of justice has an absolute weight with respect to the principle of utility (not necessarily with respect to other moral concepts). By that I meant that the union of the two concepts of justice and utility must take the form of the principle of establishing the most efficient just institution. This means that an unjust institution or law cannot be justified by an appeal to a greater net sum of advantages, and that the duty of fair play cannot be analogously overridden. An unjust institution or law or the overriding of the duty of fair play can be justified only by a greater balance of justice. I know of no way to prove this proposition. It is not proved by the analytic argument to show that the principles of justice are indeed the principles of justice. But I think it may be shown that the principle to establish the most efficient just institutions does not lead to conclusions counter to our intuitive judgments and that it is not in any way irrational. It is, moreover, something of a theoretical simplification, in that one does not have to balance justice against utility. But this simplification is no doubt not a real one, since it is as difficult to ascertain the balance of justice as anything else.[3]

[3] [Not surprisingly, Rawls' argument has met challenge from utilitarians. The utilitarian will argue that, even if it would be bad for everyone to perform some act *A* (such as breaking the law), one may still be morally justified in performing *A* if he has reasonable grounds for believing that in fact not everyone will perform *A*. It would be bad for everyone to break the law, surely, but not everyone will. It is empirically false that, in most cases, an act of disobedience on the part of one man will lead to an "epidemic" of disobedience. And, according to the utilitarian, it is morally quite permissible to take this fact into account in justifying one's disobedient conduct. An action may be unfair; but the utilitarian, unlike Rawls, will argue that it is morally permissible on grounds of utility to perform unfair or unjust actions. For a development of the utilitarian position on this issue, see the following: Richard Brandt, "Utility and the Obligation to Obey the Law," *Law and Philosophy*, ed. Sidney Hook (New York, 1964); Richard Wasserstrom, "The Obligation to Obey the Law," *U.C.L.A. Law Review*, X (May 1963), reprinted in *Essays in Legal Philosophy*, ed. Robert S. Summers (Berkeley, 1968). On the general question of resolving conflicts between justice and utility, see Brian Barry, "Justice and the Common Good," *Analysis*, Vol. 21, 1960–61, reprinted in *Political Philosophy*, ed. Anthony Quinton (Oxford, 1967). Ed.]

Sidney Hook

Social Protest and Civil Obedience

In times of moral crisis what has been accepted as common-place truth sometimes appears questionable and problematic. We have all been nurtured in the humanistic belief that in a democracy, citizens are free to disagree with a law but that so long as it remains in force, they have a *prima facie* obligation to obey it. The belief is justified on the ground that this procedure enables us to escape the twin evils of tyranny and anarchy. Tyranny is avoided by virtue of the freedom and power of dissent to win the uncoerced consent of the community. Anarchy is avoided by reliance on due process, the recognition that there is a right way to correct a wrong, and a wrong way to secure a right. To the extent that anything is demonstrable in human affairs, we have held that democracy as a political system is not viable if members systematically refused to obey laws whose wisdom or morality they dispute.

Nonetheless, during the past decade of tension and turmoil in American life there has developed a mass phenomenon of civil disobedience even among those who profess devotion to democratic ideals and institutions. This phenomenon has assumed a character similar to a tidal wave which has not yet reached its crest. It has swept from the field of race relations to the campuses of some universities, subtly altering the connotation of the term "academic." It is being systematically developed as an instrument of influencing foreign policy. It is leaving its mark on popular culture. I am told it is not only a theme of comic books but that children in our more sophisticated families no longer resort to tantrums in defying parental discipline—they go limp!

More seriously, in the wake of civil disobedience there has

This article first appeared in *The Humanist*, Fall 1967, and is reprinted by permission. Sidney Hook is Professor of Philosophy at New York University, a founder of the Congress for Cultural Freedom, and former President of the American Philosophical Association (Eastern Division). His many publications include the following books: *The Paradoxes of Freedom, Religion in a Free Society, Education for Modern Man*, and *Reason, Social Myths and Democracy*.

occasionally developed *uncivil* disobedience, sometimes as a natural psychological development, and often because of the failure of law enforcement agencies especially in the South to respect and defend legitimate expressions of social protest. The line between civil and uncivil disobedience is not only an uncertain and wavering one in practice, it has become so in theory. A recent prophet of the philosophy of the absurd in recommending civil disobedience as a form of creative disorder in a democracy cited Shay's Rebellion as an illustration. This Rebellion was uncivil to the point of bloodshed. Indeed, some of the techniques of protesting American involvement in Vietnam have departed so far from traditional ways of civil disobedience as to make it likely that they are inspired by the same confusion between civil and uncivil disobedience.

All this has made focal the perennial problems of the nature and limits of the citizen's obligation to obey the law, of the relation between the authority of conscience and the authority of the state, of the rights and duties of a democratic moral man in an immoral democratic society. The classical writings on these questions have acquired a burning relevance to the political condition of man today. I propose briefly to clarify some of these problems.

To begin with I wish to stress the point that there is no problem concerning "social protest" as such in a democracy. Our Bill of Rights was adopted not only to make protest possible but to encourage it. The political logic, the very ethos of any democracy that professes to rest, no matter how indirectly, upon freely given consent *requires* that social protest be permitted—and not only permitted but *protected* from interference by those opposed to the protest, which means protected by agencies of law enforcement.

Not social protest but *illegal* social protest constitutes our problem. It raises the question: "When, if ever, is illegal protest justified in a democratic society?" It is of the first importance to bear in mind that we are raising the question as principled democrats and humanists in a democratic society. To urge that illegal social protests, motivated by exalted ideals are sanctified in a democratic society by precedents like the Boston Tea Party, is a lapse into political illiteracy. Such actions occurred in societies in which those affected by unjust laws had no power peacefully to change them.

Further, many actions dubbed civilly disobedient by local authorities, strictly speaking, are not such at all. An action launched in violation of a local law or ordinance, and undertaken to test it, on the ground that the law itself violates state or federal law, or launched in violation of a state law in the sincerely held belief that the state law outrages the Constitution, the supreme law of the land, is not civilly disobedient. In large measure the original sympathy with which the original sit-ins were received, especially the Freedom Rides, marches, and demonstrations that flouted local Southern laws, was due to the conviction that they were constitutionally justified, in accordance with the heritage of freedom, enshrined in the Amendments, and enjoyed in other regions of the country. Practically everything the marchers did was sanctioned by the phrase of the First Amendment which upholds "the right of the people peaceably to assemble and to petition the Government for a redress of grievances." Actions of this kind may be wise or unwise, timely or untimely, but they are not civilly disobedient.

They become civilly disobedient when they are in deliberate violation of laws that have been sustained by the highest legislative and judicial bodies of the nation, e.g., income tax laws, conscription laws, laws forbidding segregation in education, and discrimination in public accommodations and employment. Another class of examples consists of illegal social protest against local and state laws that clearly do not conflict with Federal Law.

Once we grasp the proper issue, the question is asked with deceptive clarity: "Are we under an obligation in a democratic community always to obey an unjust law?" To this question Abraham Lincoln is supposed to have made the classic answer in an eloquent address on "The Perpetuation of Our Political Institution," calling for absolute and religious obedience until the unjust law is repealed.

I said that this question is asked with deceptive clarity because Lincoln, judging by his other writings and the pragmatic cast of his basic philosophy, could never have subscribed to this absolutism or meant what he seemed literally to have said. Not only are we under no moral obligation *always* to obey unjust laws, we are under no moral obligation *always* to obey a just law. One can put it more strongly: sometimes it may be necessary in the interests of the greater good to violate a just or sensible law. A man who refused to violate a sensible traffic law if it were necessary to do so to avoid a probably fatal accident would be a moral idiot. There are other values in the world besides legality or even justice, and sometimes they may be of overriding concern and weight. Everyone can imagine some situation in which the violation of some existing law is the lesser moral evil, but this does not invalidate recognition of our obligation to obey just laws.

There is a difference between disobeying a law which one approves of in general but whose application in a specific case seems wrong, and disobeying a law in protest against the injustice of the law itself. In the latter case the disobedience is open and public; in the former, not. But if the grounds of disobedience in both cases are moral considerations, there is only a difference in degree between them. The rejection, therefore, of legal absolutism or the fetishism of legality—that one is never justified in violating any law in any circumstances—is a matter of common sense.

The implications drawn from this moral commonplace by some ritualistic liberals are clearly absurd. For they have substituted for the absolutism of law something very close to the absolutism of individual conscience. Properly rejecting the view that the law, no matter how unjust, must be obeyed in all circumstances, they have taken the view that the law is to be obeyed only when the individual deems it just or when it does not outrage his conscience. Fantastic comparisons are made between those who do not act on the dictates of their conscience and those who accepted and obeyed Hitler's laws. These comparisons completely disregard the systems of law involved, the presence of alternatives of action, the differences in the behavior commanded, in degrees of complicity of guilt, in the moral costs and personal consequences of compliance and other relevant matters.

It is commendable to recognize the primacy of morality to law but unless we recognize the centrality of intelligence to morality, we stumble with blind self-righteousness into moral disaster. Because, Kant to the contrary notwithstanding, it is not wrong sometimes to lie to save a human life; because it is not wrong sometimes to kill in defense to save many from being killed, it does not follow that the moral principles: "Do not lie!" "Do not kill!" are invalid. When more than one valid principle bears on a problem of moral experience, the very fact of their conflict means that not all of them can hold unqualifiedly. One of them must be denied. The point is that such negation or violation entails upon us the obligation of justifying it, and moral justification is a matter of reasons not of conscience. The burden of proof rests on the person violating the rules. Normally, we don't have to justify telling the truth. We do have to justify *not* telling the truth. Similarly, with respect to the moral obligation of a democrat who breaches his political obligation to obey the laws of a democratic community, the resort to conscience is not enough. There must always be reasonable justification.

This is all the more true because just as we can, if challenged, give powerful reasons for the moral principle of truth-telling, so we can offer logically coercive grounds for the obligation of a democrat to obey the laws of a democracy. The grounds are many and they can be amplified beyond the passing mention we give here. It is a matter of fairness, of social utility, of peace, or ordered progress, of redeeming an implicit commitment.

There is one point, however, which has a particular relevance to the claims of those who counterpose to legal absolutism the absolutism of conscience. There is the empirically observable tendency for public disobedience to law to spread from those who occupy high moral ground to those who dwell on low ground, with consequent growth of disorder and insecurity.

Conscience by itself is not the measure of high or low moral ground. This is the work of reason. Where it functions properly the democratic process permits this resort to reason. If the man of conscience loses in the court of reason, why should he assume that the decision or the law is mistaken rather than the deliverances of his conscience?

The voice of conscience may sound loud and clear. But it may conflict at times not only with the law but with another man's conscience. Every conscientious objector to a law knows that at least one man's conscience is wrong, *viz.,* the conscience of the man who asserts that *his* conscience tells him that he must not tolerate conscientious objectors. From this if he is reasonable he should conclude that when he hears the voice of conscience, he is hearing not the voice of God, but the voice of a finite, limited man in this time and in this place, and that conscience is neither a special nor an infallible organ of apprehending moral truth, that conscience without conscientiousness, conscience which does not cap the process of critical reflective morality, is likely to be prejudice masquerading as a First Principle or a Mandate from Heaven.

The mark of an enlightened democracy is, as far as is possible with its security, to respect the religious commitment of a citizen who believes, on grounds of conscience or any other ground, that his relation to God involves duties superior to those arising from any human relation. It, therefore, exempts him from his duty as a citizen to protect his country. However, the mark of the genuine conscientious objector in a democracy is to respect the democratic process. He does not use his exemption as a political weapon to coerce where he has failed to convince or persuade. Having failed to influence national policy by rational means within the law, in the political processes open to him in a free society, he cannot justifiably try to defeat that policy by resorting to obstructive techniques outside the law and still remain a democrat.

It is one thing on grounds of conscience or religion to plead exemption from the duty of serving one's country when drafted. It is quite another to adopt harassing techniques to prevent others from volunteering or responding to the call of duty. It is one thing to oppose American involvement in Vietnam by teach-ins, petitions, electoral activity. It is quite another to attempt to stop troop trains: to take possession of the premises of draft boards where policies are not made; to urge recruits to sabotage their assignments and feign illness to win discharge. The first class of actions falls within the sphere of legitimate social protest; the second class is implicitly insurrectionary since it is directed against the authority of a democratic government which it seeks to overthrow not by argument and discussion but by resistance—albeit passive resistance.

Nonetheless, since we have rejected legal absolutism we must face the possibility that in protest on ethical grounds individuals may refuse to obey some law which they regard as uncommonly immoral or uncommonly foolish. If they profess to be democrats, their behavior must scrupulously respect the following conditions:

First, it must be nonviolent—peaceful not only in form but in actuality. After all, the protesters are seeking to dramatize a great evil that the community allegedly has been unable to overcome because of complacency or moral weakness. Therefore, they must avoid the guilt of imposing hardship or harm on others who in the nature of the case can hardly be responsible for the situation under protest. Passive resistance should not be utilized merely as a safer or more effective strategy than active resistance of imposing their wills on others.

Secondly, resort to civil disobedience is never morally legitimate where other methods of remedying the evil complained of are available. Existing grievance procedures should be used. No grievance procedures were available to the southern Negroes. The Courts often shared the prejudices of the community and offered no relief, not even minimal protection. But such procedures *are* available in the areas of industry and education. For example, where charges against students are being heard such procedures may result in the dismissal of the charges not the students. Or the faculty on appeal may decide to suspend the rules rather than the students. To jump the gun to civil disobedience in bypassing these procedures is tell-tale evidence that those who are calling the shots are after other game than preserving the rights of students.

Thirdly, those who resort to civil disobedience are duty bound to accept the legal sanctions and punishments imposed by the laws. Attempts to evade and escape them not only involve a betrayal of the community, but erode the moral foundations of civil disobedience itself. Socrates' argument in the *Crito* is valid only on democratic premises. The rationale of the protesters is the hope that the pain and hurt and indignity they voluntarily accept will stir their fellow citizens to compassion, open their minds to second thoughts, and move them to undertake the necessary healing action. When, however, we observe the heroics of defiance being followed by the dialectics of legal evasion, we question the sincerity of the action.

Fourth, civil disobedience is unjustified if a major moral issue is not clearly at stake. Differences about negotiable details that can easily be settled with a little patience should not be fanned into a blaze of illegal opposition.

Fifth, where intelligent men of good will and character differ on large and complex moral issues, discussion and agitation are more appropriate than civilly disobedient action. Those who feel strongly about animal rights and regard the consumption of animal flesh as foods as morally evil would have a just cause for civil disobedience if *their* freedom to obtain other food was threatened. They would have no moral right to resort to similar action to prevent their fellow citizens from consuming meat. Similarly with fluoridation.

Sixth, where civil disobedience is undertaken, there must be some rhyme and reason in the time, place, and targets selected. If one is convinced, as I am not, that the Board of Education of New York City is remiss in its policy of desegregation, what is the point of dumping garbage on bridges to produce traffic jams that seriously discomfort commuters who have not the remotest connection with educational policies in New York? Such action can only obstruct the progress of desegregation in the communities of Long Island. Gandhi, who inspired the civil disobedience movement in the twentieth century, was a better tactician than many who invoke his name but ignore his teachings. When he organized his campaign of civil disobedience against the Salt Tax, he marched with his followers to the sea to make salt. He did not hold up food trains or tie up traffic.

Finally, there is such a thing as historical timing. Democrats who resort to civil disobedience must ask themselves whether the cumulative consequences of their action may in the existing climate of opinion undermine the peace and order on which the effective exercise of other human rights depend. This is a cost which one may be willing to pay but which must be taken into the reckoning.

These observations in the eyes of some defenders of the philosophy of civil disobedience are far from persuasive. They regard them as evading the political realities. The political realities, it is asserted, do not provide meaningful channels for the legitimate expression of dissent. The "Establishment" is too powerful or indifferent to be moved. Administrations are voted into office that are not bound by their election pledges. The right to form minority parties is hampered by unconstitutional voting laws. What does even "the right of the people to present petitions for the redress of grievances" amount to if it does not carry with it the right to have those petitions paid attention to, at least to have them read, if not acted upon?

No, the opposing argument runs on. Genuine progress does not come by enactment of laws, by appeals to the good will or conscience of one's fellow citizens, but only by obstructions which interfere with the functioning of the system itself, by actions whose nuisance value is so high that the Establishment finds it easier to be decent and yield to demands than to be obdurate and oppose them. The time comes, as one student leader of the civilly disobedient Berkeley students advised, "when it is necessary for you to throw your bodies upon the wheels and gears and levers and bring the machine to a grinding halt." When one objects that such obstruction, as a principle of political action, is almost sure to produce chaos, and that it is unnecessary and undesirable in a democracy, the retort is made: "Amen, if only this were a democracy, how glad we would be to stop!"

It is characteristic of those who argue this way to define the presence or absence of the democratic process by whether or not *they* get their political way, and not by the presence or absence of democratic institutional processes. The rules of the game exist to enable them to win and if they lose that's sufficient proof the game is rigged and dishonest. The sincerity with which the position is held is no evidence whatsoever of its coherence. The right to petition does not carry with it the right to be heard, if that means influence on those to whom it is addressed. What would they do if they received incompatible petitions from two different and hostile groups of petitioning citizens? The right of petition gives one a chance to persuade, and the persuasion must rest on the power of words, on the effective appeal to emotion, sympathy, reason, and logic. Petitions are weapons of criticism, and their failure does not justify appeal to other kinds of weapons.

It is quite true that some local election laws do hamper minority groups in the organization of political parties; but there is always the right of appeal to the Courts. Even if this fails there is a possibility of influencing other political parties. It is difficult but so long as one is free to publish and speak, it can be done. If a group is unsuccessful in moving a majority by the weapons of criticism, in a democracy it may resort to peaceful measures of obstruction, provided it is willing to accept punishment for its obstructionist behavior. But these objections are usually a preface to some form of elitism or moral snobbery which is incompatible with the very grounds given in defending the right of civil disobedience on the part of democrats in a democracy.

All of the seven considerations listed above are cautionary, not categorical. We have ruled out only two positions—blind obedience to any and all laws in a democracy, and unreflective violation of laws at the behest of individual consciences. Between these two obviously unacceptable extremes, there is a spectrum of views which shade into each other. Intelligent persons can differ on their application to specific situations. These differences will reflect different assessments of the historical mood of a culture, of the proper timing of protest and acquiescence, and of what the most desirable emphasis and direction of our teaching should be in order to extend "the blessing of liberty" as we preserve "domestic tranquility."

Without essaying the role of a prophet, here is my reading of the needs of the present. It seems to me that the Civil Rights Acts of 1964 and the Voting Acts of 1965 mark a watershed in the history of social and civil protest in the U.S. Upon their enforcement a great many things we hold dear depend, especially those causes in behalf of which in the last decade so many movements of social protest were launched. We must recall that it was the emasculation of the 15th Amendment in the South which kept the Southern Negro in a state of virtual peonage. The prospect of enforcement of the new civil rights legislation is a function of many factors—most notably the law-abiding behavior of the hitherto recalcitrant elements in the southern white communities. Their *uncivil,* violent disobedience has proved unavailing. We need not fear this so much as that they will adopt the strategies and techniques of the civil disobedience itself in their opposition to long-delayed and decent legislation to make the ideals of American democracy a greater reality.

On the other hand, I think the movement of civil disobedience, as distinct from legal protest, in regions of the country in which Negroes have made slow but substantial advances are not likely to make new gains commensurate with the risks. Those risks are that what is begun as civil disobedience will be perverted by extremists into uncivil disobedience, and alienate large numbers who have firmly supported the cause of freedom.

One of the unintended consequences of the two World Wars is that in many ways they strengthened the position of the Negroes and all other minorities in American political life. We do not need another, a third World War, to continue the process of liberation. We can do it in peace—without war and without civil war. The Civil Rights and Voting Acts of 1964 and 1965 are far in advance of the actual situation in the country where discrimination is so rife. Our present task is to bring home and reinforce popular consciousness of the fact that those who violate their provisions are violating the highest law of the land, and that their actions are outside the law. Therefore, our goal must *now* be to build up and strengthen a mood of respect for the law, for civil obedience to laws, even by those who deem them unwise or who opposed them in the past. Our hope is that those who abide by the law may learn not only to tolerate them but, in time, as their fruits develop, to accept them. To have the positive law on the side of right and justice is to have a powerful weapon that makes for voluntary compliance—but only if the *reasonableness* of the *prima facie* obligation to obey the law is recognized.

To one observer at least, that reasonableness is being more and more disregarded in this country. The current mood is one of growing indifference to and disregard of even the reasonable legalities. The headlines from New York to California tell the story. I am not referring to the crime rate which has made frightening strides, nor to the fact that some of our metropolitan centers have become dangerous jungles. I refer to a growing mood toward law generally, something comparable to the attitude toward the Volstead Act during the Prohibition era. The mood is more diffuse today. To be law-abiding in some circles is to be "a square."

In part, the community itself has been responsible for the emergence of this mood. This is especially true in those states which have failed to abolish the *unreasonable* legalities, particularly in the fields of marriage, divorce, birth control, sex behavior, therapeutic abortion, voluntary euthanasia, and other intrusions on the right of privacy. The failure to repeal foolish laws, which makes morally upright individuals legal offenders, tends to generate skepticism and indifference toward observing the reasonable legalities.

This mood must change if the promise of recent civil rights legislation is to be realized. Respect for law today can give momentum to the liberal upswing of the political and social pendulum in American life. In a democracy we cannot make an absolute of obedience to law or to anything else except "the moral obligation to be intelligent," but more than ever we must stress that dissent and opposition—the oxygen of free society —be combined with civic obedience, and that on moral grounds it express itself as legal dissent and legal opposition.

Jeffrie G. Murphy

The Vietnam War and
the Right of Resistance

64 The contemporary American government generates a pervasive and substantial amount of moral agony among its citizens. And this is unfortunate. For one of the primary functions of a constitutional representative government is to provide a generally just and agreeable social decision procedure for political policy which will make moral confrontation between a citizen and his government rare. This leaves the citizen free to pursue his own limited aims—free to seek his own peace and happiness in the reasonable expectation that the rules under which he lives will resolve political matters, if not in the very best way, at least in a way that is neither highly unjust nor highly productive of human misery.

But this situation, though it is the ideal envisioned in democratic theory, is clearly nowhere near the reality which currently presents itself to us. Many reasonable and sensitive men find it increasingly difficult to continue recognizing a moral obligation to abide by the results of the decision procedures of the state; for the exercise of these procedures seems to them increasingly unjust, arbitrary, deceitful, and secret. Thus it is that they feel the moral necessity of subjecting every single act of our government to minute scrutiny. And such necessity compels them to ignore more and more those private satisfactions of the good life which democracy is supposed to secure for each citizen. For the pursuit of private goals, in the present context, strikes them as unjustifiably narrow and selfish. Such an attitude is reflected in the refusal of many students to go on with "business as usual" and in their decisions to abandon their studies and careers for direct political action.[1]

This essay was delivered at a teach-in at the University of Minnesota (1967) and to an undergraduate honors colloquium at the University of Michigan (1968). It is published here (with updating of references) for the first time. All rights reserved.

[1] For many students, such slogans are surely nothing but a rationalizing mask for indolence or even psychopathy. But for many others, they are just as surely an expression of conscience and moral sensitivity.

Such a state of affairs sets the stage for a more radical kind of resistance or civil disobedience than that found, for example, in the early Southern sit-ins led by Martin Luther King, Jr., and others. The disobedience practiced there typically involved a faith in the ultimate integrity of the legal system. A claim made by those in disobedience was that their actions were really legal, that they were of such a nature that—even if prohibited by local statute—they would ultimately be upheld as protected by our Constitution. Present-day radical resistance has no such faith. Those who, with Benjamin Spock and others, advocate or practice resistance to the operation of Selective Service may not be in the least dissuaded by any Supreme Court ruling that such resistance is not constitutionally protected. So much the worse, they may argue, for the Court and (for the present instance) the Constitution.[2]

It is hard to overestimate the gravity of this response to government, for it strikes at the roots of the very idea of law. It is surely a response to which a reasonable man will only slowly and regretfully come. But sometimes, as the history of Nazi Germany has surely taught us, it may have to come. My purpose here is to sketch one set of conditions (possibly satisfied, in my judgment, by our government's conduct of the Vietnam War) in which such a radical response may be claimed as a *moral* right.[3] No claim will be made that these are the only such conditions or that, having a right to resist, the citizen *ought* to exercise it. Whether one should resist the law obviously depends, among other things, upon the complex circumstances surrounding the particular case—for example, whether resistance is likely to advance one's aims, whether it will result in the harming of people, whether it will provoke repression, and

---

[2] There is, of course, an even more radical response which I shall not discuss here—namely, the response of the *revolutionary*. As I understand the intentions of people like Dr. Spock, they are not revolutionary. Many of those who advocate draft resistance do so, not because they find the American system of constitutional democracy evil in principle, but because they believe that the present government has not itself been loyal to the rules and ideals of that very system. Thus they desire to restore the system to health. The revolutionary, on the other hand, finds the very principles of the system corrupt and wants to overthrow them entirely. Revolutionary resistance raises interesting and important problems, but they are not problems of civil disobedience.

[3] The question of whether there might also be a legal or quasi-legal basis for such a right is discussed in Ronald Dworkin's "On Not Prosecuting Civil Disobedience," *New York Review of Books*, June 6, 1968. My interest will be in the person who resists Selective Service (refuses induction, for example) because he believes that the Vietnam War is illegal. Even if the war is illegal, it is not clear that this will entail the illegality of the draft laws (the laws actually resisted). Thus the draft resister, even if he bases his resistance in part on a belief that the war is illegal, will not necessarily be claiming a legal right to resist.

(so important but so often forgotten) whether it will harden or soften the hearts of men—whether it will advance or retard the cause of civilization and human decency.[4] My aim is simply to show that there are cases in which resistance, no matter how open to criticism on other grounds, cannot fairly be criticized as a violation of one's solemn moral obligation to obey the law of the land.

Pursuing certain implications of Enlightenment political theory (such as that of Locke and Kant), I want to suggest that a citizen is morally obligated to obey the law as such only if the government under which he lives satisfies what I shall call the obligation of reciprocity. A less technical name for this obligation is simply "fair play."[5] Law and government form a system of social benefits which is made possible only as a result of mutual forbearances. The benefits I enjoy are possible only because of the sacrifices (and obedience *is* a sacrifice) of others. Therefore it is an obligation of reciprocity (since it is only fair) that I bear the necessary burdens of obedience when my turn comes. I expect others to obey laws of which they do not approve, and so it is only fair that I be at least *prima facie* prepared to do likewise. Such reciprocity is required to make law and government possible; for if everyone acted solely on his own private judgment, there would be no sense to the notion of social rules or of the rule of law as a social decision procedure. When men start acting as judges with respect to their own controversies, the very concepts "judge" and "law" operate without sense. For if I propose to serve as my own judge and legislator, and thus to refuse allegiance to rules which conflict with my own private judgment, I am claiming a liberty for myself which could not (consistent with the maintenance of a just

4 Michael Walzer has argued that some important considerations relevant to this question are the commitments that one has made to fellow members of secondary associations like political groups or religious sects. When these secondary associations have a "claim to primacy," then one's commitments can yield a *prima facie* obligation to disobey those rules of the state which are in conflict with the rules or ideals of the association. See his "The Obligation to Disobey," *Ethics*, April 1967. This may also be found in *Political Theory and Social Change*, edited by David Spitz (New York, 1967).

5 I am here drawing on a theory elaborated by John Rawls in his "Legal Obligation and the Duty of Fair Play" in *Law and Philosophy*, edited by Sidney Hook (New York, 1964). See also my "Violence and the Rule of Law," *Ethics*, July 1970, and my "In Defense of Obligation," in *Nomos XII: Political and Legal Obligation*, edited by J. Roland Pennock and John W. Chapman (New York, 1970). The theory outlined is, of course, a version of the "social contract" theory found in the thought of such earlier philosophers as Hobbes, Locke, Kant, Rousseau, and Socrates (in Plato's *Crito*). Rawls has outlined a theory of civil disobedience in his "The Justification of Civil Disobedience," in *Civil Disobedience: Theory and Practice*, edited by Hugo Adam Bedau (New York, 1969).

rule of law) be extended to all other people. And this is a sign that I am proposing to act in an unfair or unjust way. To put the point very crudely, people who sincerely believe in the rule of law and in democracy must be prepared, on occasion, to *lose.* This does not mean that one must always, no matter what the circumstances, accept defeat. But it does mean that one has a *prima facie* obligation, based on reciprocity, to accept defeat—that is, the burden of moral proof lies on the man who proposes not to accept defeat. We are all inclined to talk about the sanctity of the law when *others* whose views we do not share (segregationists perhaps) seek to resist, and thus it is only fair that we find such appeals at least relevant (if not always decisive) when made against a cause like draft resistance of which we may approve.

Having outlined the obligation of reciprocity, I want now to insist on something that may be regarded as controversial— namely, that this obligation falls most heavily upon the *government itself.*[6] For if an individual citizen fails to obey the law, the damage he can do is minimal. We also have institutions to deal with him. Criminal punishment, after all, is an institution which functions to keep most citizens from unfairly suffering as a result of disobedience by others. But government is not in the position of the average citizen. Government holds a near monopoly on the force in a given society, and this makes it both highly dangerous and invulnerable. Thus its deviations from the rule of law present a threat to the integrity of society far beyond that posed by any individual citizen. Even more important, of course, is the fact that government—especially constitutional representative government—has the solemn trust of preserving the rule of law. It must call upon its citizens for

---

[6] Hobbes and Kant, for example denied this. (For Kant's views on legal obligation and resistance, see his "Concerning the Saying: That May be True in Theory but not in Practice," and for a discussion of his views see my *Kant: The Philosophy of Right* [London, 1970].) The legal positions of government officials and average citizens are, of course, different in certain important respects. Government officials and average citizens, though many of their legal obligations (not to drive over the speed limit, for example) overlap, also have nonoverlapping obligations. The President does not have a legal obligation to serve in the army, but he does have a legal obligation not to embark the nation on a war in violation of the Constitution. The average citizen, on the other hand, has a legal obligation to serve in the army but does not have a legal obligation to make war only in accord with the Constitution; for the citizen is not in a legal position to conduct war at all. The important point for our purposes, however, is that both government officials and the citizens have a common *moral* obligation—namely, to support the rule of law. This means, among other things, that both government officials and citizens, if they are indeed loyal to the principles of constitutional democracy, must recognize an obligation to pursue their own ends only in so far as doing so is consistent with their respective legal obligations.

obedience; and, if it is to be morally persuasive and not merely coercive in doing this, its own hands must be clean. Consider an analogy with a game: Deviations from rules by players make the game difficult, but this difficulty is in principle remediable. Deviations from the rules by the *umpire,* however, make the game impossible—make the game cease to operate as a system of rules at all.

Thus government, if it is to be justified in calling upon its citizens to honor an obligation to obey the law of the land, must be able to show that it has met its own obligations in that regard—that it has satisfied its own obligation of reciprocity or fair dealing. Government, after all, is not a good in itself. It is useful only insofar as it provides us with justice and the kind of security that living under a system of rules can make possible. When government deviates from those rules, its value is eroded. And with this erosion goes government's justification and its moral claim on our obedience.

What is the practical upshot of all this? I should like to suggest the following: When it can be demonstrated (and the burden of proof is on the citizen) that the government has violated its obligation of reciprocity by ignoring its own legal duties and limitations, then the government has no right to call upon the citizen to satisfy his own end of the social bargain. In such circumstances the citizen is *not* morally obligated to obey the law as such, and thus he may legitimately claim a right to resist. A believer in the rule of law and in democracy must be willing to accept defeat, yes, but only if the defeat is *just*—that is, only if it results from the fair use of fair procedures.

Now, as I have previously suggested, having a *right* to resist does not entail that one *ought* to resist. This depends upon a large number of other moral considerations—one being whether resistance will tend to restore or further deteriorate the rule of law.[7] Also, a right to resist does not make a citizen morally free to break any law he happens to feel like breaking. For even though a government may deal unfairly with its citizens in some areas, it may deal with them quite fairly in others. And surely there are sufficient moral reasons for obeying some rules (such as "Do not murder") regardless of the legal status of those rules, for some actions are wrong in themselves (*mala in se* and not just *mala prohibita*). Even when talk of resistance

---

[7] This will depend, in large measure, on the *manner* in which the resistance takes place. Simple refusal of induction (and consequent jail or exile), for example, will tend to threaten the rule of law to a much lesser extent than violent demonstrations and the repression they often provoke.

seems appropriate, in other words, reasonable men should still draw distinctions.

Having outlined a theoretical structure, I should now like to apply it to a concrete case—one of a current importance almost impossible to overestimate. The case is the Vietnam War and the right of resistance (draft resistance, for example) to that war. In my judgment the following claims (none of them unreasonable to believe) provide a *prima facie* case for a right to such resistance:[8]

1. The war began as the private adventure of the President. It was not and never has been, as the Constitution requires, declared by Congress.[9]

2. The war is arguably in violation of treaties and the United Nations Charter—all of which are supposedly legally binding on our national action.[10]

[8] I say *"prima facie* case" for the following reason: It is a matter of empirical and legal investigation, and not of philosophy, whether or not the following claims have indeed been established as facts. I (admittedly a nonexpert) tend to be persuaded by the evidence in their favor. If others are not persuaded, then we know where we disagree and how to develop our discussion. Thus the claims should at least serve to illustrate, even for a person who is unconvinced, what is relevant for applying the theory and how an application of that theory might look. For opposing views, see Sidney Hook, "Social Protest and Civil Obedience," *The Humanist,* Fall 1967; Abe Fortas, *Concerning Dissent and Civil Disobedience* (New York, 1968); and Judge Charles E. Wyzanski, Jr., "On Civil Disobedience," *Atlantic Monthly,* February, 1968. Fortas argues that the legal channels for redress of grievances are adequate, and Hook suggests that most people who complain that the channels are not adequate are simply angry at not having gotten their own way. I shall suggest that the evidence for this complaint is much stronger than Hook is willing to admit.

[9] Nicholas Katzenbach, former Assistant Secretary of State, once called the Gulf of Tonkin Resolution a "functional equivalent" of a declaration of war. In addition to wondering what this phrase might mean, it is important to note the following: There is evidence, much of it brought out in hearings conducted by Senator Fulbright, that the Johnson administration seduced Congress into passing this resolution by the presentation of misdescribed and even fabricated incidents of "attacks" on U.S. ships by the North Vietnamese. See Peter Dale Scott, "Tonkin Bay: Was There a Conspiracy?" *New York Review of Books,* July 29, 1970. Considering the length of the conflict and the number of casualties in Vietnam, it would be hard to deny that it really is properly called a "war" and that it is thus subject to Article I, section 8, of the Constitution, which was intended as an explicit restriction upon the power of the executive to initiate war on his own prerogative —such a power being then enjoyed by the British sovereign.

[10] This is argued in, among other places, the *Memorandum of Law of Lawyers' Committee on American Policy toward Vietnam,* read into the *Congressional Record* by Senator Morse on September 23, 1965. Defenders of the international legality of the war may, for example, cite the SEATO treaty as providing authorization for the war. The legal issues here are extremely complex, and this is the primary reason why so many concerned citizens desire a court ruling on the legality of the war. In the absence of such a ruling, what is the citizen to do except form his own reasoned individual judgment on the matter? For a review of the legal issues, see the following: Richard A. Falk, *The Six Legal Dimensions of the Vietnam War* (Princeton, 1968); Richard A. Falk, ed., *The Vietnam War and International Law* (Princeton, Vol. I [1968] and Vol. II [1969]); Roger H. Hull, *Law and Vietnam*

3. *The Selective Service, which is the major instrument supporting the war, has been used for the illegal purpose of punishing dissent. Even Justice Fortas, no friend of civil disobedients, once called its former director "a law unto himself."*

4. *The war was escalated contrary to all campaign pledges of President Johnson. Democracy demands the periodic review of officials and their policies. When these officials refuse to be candid about their policies, then the democratic process is made a sham. For no informed choice of consent is then possible.*

5. *The federal courts (including the Supreme Court) have refused to decide cases where citizens have challenged the legality of the war—typically by raising points 1 and 2 above. Thus a promised channel for the legal redress of grievances has, for all practical purposes, been closed.*[11]

6. *The war is an ideological war. That is, it does not appear to be a war in defense of those national benefits we should all perhaps be willing to maintain by our sacrifice. Rather it is more like a religious war—a war to stamp out the heresy of Communism. The Cold Warriors behind it are, of course, entitled to their religious beliefs. But are they entitled to sacrifice*

(New York, 1968); *In the Name of America: the conduct of the war in Vietnam by the armed forces of the United States as shown by published reports, compared with the laws of war binding on the United States Government and on its citizens,* Clergy and Laymen Concerned about Vietnam (New York, 1968); and Telford Taylor, *Nuremberg and Vietnam: An American Tragedy* (New York, 1970).

[11] Justice Fortas, in his *Concerning Dissent and Civil Disobedience* (New York, 1968), condemns radicals for not using legitimate channels for the redress of their grievances. And yet, while on the Supreme Court, he was one of the justices who refused to hear cases on the war. This makes his pleas for the use of "legitimate channels" sound rather hollow. (The important cases here are *Mitchell v. United States,* 369 F. 2d 323 (1966), cert. denied, 386 U.S. 972 (1967) and *Mora v. McNamara,* reported as *Luftig v. McNamara,* 252 F. Supp. 819 (D.D.C. 1966), aff'd 373 F. 2d 664 (D.C. Cir.), cert. denied sub nom., *Mora v. McNamara,* 389 U.S. 934 (1967)—Douglas dissenting in *Mitchell,* Douglas and Stewart dissenting in *Mora.*) In refusing to hear such cases, the Court typically relies on the "political question" doctrine—that is, that questions concerning the war are political in the sense that, rather than being purely legal or constitutional, they are properly to be decided by some other branch of government. This strikes many as a subterfuge which allows the Court to avoid its true responsibilities—particularly when the Court fails even to give a *reason* for refusing to hear the case. For a probing discussion of this problem, with application to civil disobedience, see Graham Hughes, "Civil Disobedience and the Political Question Doctrine," *New York University Law Review,* LXIII, No. 1 (March 1968), pp. 1–19. For a discussion of Hughes' article, see Stephen Wexler, "The 'Political Question' Doctrine: A Decision Not to Decide" and Kai Nielsen, "The 'Political Question' Doctrine," both in *Ethics,* October 1968. Hughes' paper was presented at the International Philosophy Year Conference at Brockport in 1968 and was sharply criticized by Justice Tom Clark. Clark's paper and a reprinting of Hughes' may be found in *Ethics and Social Justice,* edited by Howard E. Kiefer and Milton K. Munitz (Albany, 1970).

others for those beliefs? "Here is a cause I believe in; now you *go out and die for it" is not a very persuasive argument.*[12]

These claims, of course, are not new. Neither do they constitute all the important objections which can be made against the war. But the issues they raise constitute so great a threat to our constitutional democracy that they cannot be repeated too many times.[13] For these particular six points, in my judgment, provide evidence that our government in the present context has violated its obligation of reciprocity to the citizens. They provide evidence that the war has been instigated and conducted in violation of the law of the land, of the very principles which define our form of government. The government itself has perhaps been engaged in resistance to law.[14]

Now in my view, *if* these claims are indeed established as facts, the implication is clear: Those who oppose the war by resistance to Selective Service may not fairly be charged with violating their moral obligation to obey the law of the land. For a condition of that obligation has been violated by government and, in so doing, government has forfeited its moral right to call upon citizens for obedience in this area. It can and will

[12] This is relevant to the issue raised in point 1. There is some justification, in the modern world of nuclear missiles, for allowing the President to respond to attack without consulting Congress for a formal declaration of war. But it would be difficult to support a claim that the Vietnam War posed this kind of "crisis" problem.

[13] Even if these claims are false, it is a danger merely to have so many people *believe* that they are true. Government, to be respected, must not even give the *illusion* of arbitrariness and tyranny. A government can, of course, meticulously adhere to legal procedure and still enact policies that lie beyond the limit of moral tolerance—e.g. genocide. I should certainly want to say that, in such circumstances, it is right (even obligatory) for the citizen to resist. However, to argue this point would require another paper.

[14] Points 4 through 6 are more complex than the earlier three. For the claim made in the first three is that a reasonably clear legal obligation has been violated. The claim made by the latter three is that the government, though not violating a clear legal obligation, is acting so as to show lack of respect for the ideals of democracy and constitutional procedure. To use one of Kant's favorite metaphors, they show adherence to the letter but not to the spirit of the law. The President is not legally obligated to be honest in his statements of policy, and the court is not legally obligated to hear important constitutional cases. But surely presidential deceit and court inaction are not consistent with the ideals which constitutional democracy is supposed to maintain. And on the obligation to serve in wars, the following observation of Hobbes is instructive: "When the defence of the commonwealth, requireth at once the help of all that are able to bear arms, every one is obliged; because otherwise the institution of the commonwealth, which they have not the purpose, or courage to preserve, was in vain" (*Leviathan,* Part 2, Chapter 21). Is it really plausible to maintain that ideological wars, like the Vietnam War, can be fitted into this model of self-defense? A belief that the model does apply must lie behind the remarks of those who condemn as cowards and traitors all those who will not serve in Vietnam.

force them to obey (or face jail or exile), but it has forfeited its *moral* claim on them. And moral claims, in a democracy, are the most important kind.

It should be clear that I have not been concerned to advocate or recommend civil disobedience or draft resistance, for a *prima facie* case for a *right* to resist is a long way from a *conclusive* case for a *duty* to resist. What I am most concerned to advocate is government's responsibility for giving the same meticulous attention to its legal obligations that it demands of citizens.

In times when government appears to exceed its own legal limitations and flaunt the rule of law, decent people who truly believe in the rule of law may be classed as "criminals." But such a classification is terribly misleading when applied to many of the current draft resisters—particularly those who have been nonviolent. Perhaps they have merely believed and acted upon what they have always been taught and what ought to be true: that America is a government of laws and not of men.[15]

---

[15] It is not to be hoped that considerations such as these will have any practical influence during time of war. But when the war is over, and passions have calmed, we should surely be willing to face up to what has been at the very least the moral and legal *ambiguity* of the whole enterprise. So doing, we should seriously consider granting amnesty to those whose consciences have forced them into jail or exile—allowing them to re-enter the community with dignity. To require of a man that he invite the personal disintegration that may result from acting against his conscience is an evil that a decent government should always seek to avoid. It should require this, if at all, only when the necessity is clear. In circumstances of ambiguity, the benefit of the doubt should be resolved in favor of the individual and his conscience. Some radicals would do well to remember this point when they are tempted to self-righteous condemnation of all soldiers.

Christian Bay

Civil Disobedience: Prerequisite for Democracy in Mass Society

During a recent debate on the war in Vietnam an irate member of the audience demanded to know if I was in favor of civil disobedience. My reply was "Yes, on some occasions." He sat down in silence, with a broad grin. Nothing else that I said from then on was worth taking seriously, só far as he was concerned. I might as well have come out in favor of arson. And I am sure many in the audience felt as he did.

This widespread tendency to recoil from the very concept of disobedience, even passive and presumably nonviolent disobedience, in a society priding itself on its liberties, is a measure of the degree of stability, if not immunity to real social change, that has been achieved by the present socioeconomic and political system in the United States.

To the spiritual fathers of the American democracy, most notably John Locke and Thomas Jefferson, it seemed evident that any liberty-loving people should have the right to stage even a bloody revolution against a tyrannical government; by comparison, the remedy of nonviolent civil disobedience would seem a mild brew indeed.

Among the most forceful counter-norms, or norms tending to lead many of us to reject a *priori* the very thought of civil disobedience, is another Lockian principle: the sanctity of the

From *Political Theory and Social Change*, edited by David Spitz. Reprinted by Permission of the Publishers, Atherton Press, Inc. Copyright © 1967, Atherton Press, Inc., New York. All Rights Reserved. Christian Bay is Professor and Head of the Department of Political Science, University of Alberta (Edmonton). His writings in political theory include "Civil Disobedience" (*International Encyclopedia of the Social Sciences*, 1967) and *The Structure of Freedom* (New York, 1964, 1958).

rule of law. Spokesmen for our academic as well as our political and economic establishments are for obvious reasons far happier with this part of Locke's theory of civil government.

Now, the classical writings of our democratic heritage, not unlike the Bible or the classical Marxist literature, can be used to prove the legitimacy of almost anything, and therefore, more critically viewed, of almost nothing. This point should be particularly poignant for those who have followed, during the last decades, developments in research and theory in the field of political behavior. For reasons of convenience and perhaps of habit as well, it has remained orthodox for our colleagues to proclaim their fealty to our democratic way of life (some, indeed, seem to feel that we are entitled to force other nations, too, to be guided by our example); and this fealty has remained unshaken, by and large, by the wealth of data that have come forth to demonstrate the wide and growing gulf between most of the classical ideals of democracy and what goes on in its name in today's mass societies.

Let us return to the part of our democratic heritage of particular concern here: the insistence on the sanctity of the rule of law. Now, a strong case for exalting the law (and indirectly, the lawyer) can be made from my own political ground of commitment to no system but to the sanctity of life, and the freedoms necessary for living,[1] *insofar as* laws (and lawyers) are to operate to protect all human lives, with priority for those most badly in need of protection. But to claim a corresponding sanctity for the laws that we have today, which, as in *every* state to a considerable extent, operate in the service of those who are privileged and influential in our socioeconomic order, seems to me to constitute an outright fraud at the expense of all the political innocents, unless one can claim for oneself, too, the innocence of not knowing any significant part of our modern behavioral literature.

At best a claim can be made that general obedience to the law is a lesser evil than general disobedience, which could well lead to much violence and conceivably even to a return to a Hobbesian state of nature. But this surely is a false issue, for no society has ever known either general obedience or general anarchy. Most of us have become trained, as generations of our ancestors have before us, to obey almost all laws almost by instinct, and certainly by habit if not by conviction. Others have become conditioned to breaking laws, frequently for reasons

---

[1] See below, section III. This position is developed at greater length in my *The Structure of Fredom* (New York, 1964, 1958).

of stunted growth on account of emotional as well as socio-economic deprivation.

Democracy has not yet been achieved, at least not in any real sense, as we shall see, in the modern world. If so, then the most familiar justifications demanding obedience to "democratically enacted" laws would seem to have no firm foundation. For the argument that every law represents the will of all, or the will of the majority, is empirically false; so is the argument that all laws aim at serving the common good. So is, as we have seen, the argument that disobedience to *any* law will promote anarchy.

Yet it obviously will not do, either, to assert that all laws can be ignored, or that any particular law can be obeyed or disobeyed as a matter of convenience. Nobody in his right mind will support all disobedience, however "civil," regardless of the issues involved. The question to be tackled, then, is not whether, but when and on what grounds civil disobedience can be justified.

My point of departure is essentially Locke's: Respect for the rule of law, or for the democratic processes that produce our laws, clearly must be contingent on and limited by standards for judging either the caliber of these processes or the purposes they promote; or, more precisely, by standards for judging how well these processes promote the purposes of politics. The *fundamental* purpose of politics, as I see it, is not to perpetuate a given political order but to protect human life and basic human rights. It cannot, if I may rub the point in, be the legitimizing purpose of politics or of government to perpetuate a political order that is democratic in name but in fact serves primarily to bolster privileges, not to equalize rights—as does ours and surely every other political order achieved till now.

The course of my argument in the remainder of this chapter will be as follows: first (II) comes a definition and a discussion of the concept of civil disobedience; next (III) a very brief statement of my own normative position, affirming the value of freedom and, only secondarily, of democracy as an aim; and then (IV) a discussion of the increasing chasm between current realities and the classical aims of democracy. I shall next (V) try to show how an expansion of the role of civil disobedience would, if anything could, turn the trend around, so that we might hope to move toward rather than away from democracy; and, finally (VI), I shall argue how essential civil disobedience is for the liberation of the individual as a political citizen—as a man and as a sharer of the burdens and benefits of politics. Since "real" democracy would require "real" citizens, this argument, too, will support the case for civil disobedience as a prerequisite for achieving something approximating democracy in modern societies.

II

"Civil disobedience" will here refer to any act or process of public defiance of a law or policy enforced by established governmental authorities, insofar as the action is premeditated, understood by the actor(s) to be illegal or of contested legality, carried out and persisted in for limited public ends, and by way of carefully chosen and limited means.

The notion of *disobedience* presupposes the concept of a norm to be disobeyed; typically a legal norm, but in any event a norm which is assumed by *some* people in power to be authoritative in the sense that transgressions would be expected to lead to punishment in one form or another. Disobedience can be active or passive; it can be a matter of doing what is prohibited or of failing to do what is required. But mere noncompliance is not enough; the action or nonaction must be openly insisted on if it is to qualify as civil disobedience, as the concept is interpreted here. For example, failure to vote in a country in which there is a legal obligation to vote does not in itself constitute civil disobedience; one would have to state in public that one does not intend to comply with the particular law; typically but not necessarily, one would publicly encourage others, too, to disobey.

The act of disobedience must be illegal, or at least be deemed illegal by powerful adversaries, and the actor must know this, if it is to be considered an act of civil disobedience.[2] Note the distinction between *conscientious objection* to military service and civil disobedience in countries that permit exemptions from otherwise obligatory service for reasons of conscience. The conscientious objector engages in civil disobedience only if he knowingly and explicitly objects to military service on grounds not recognized by the law, or in a country that makes no exceptions for reasons of conscience.

"Civil" is the more ambiguous of the two terms. At least five different meanings would appear plausible, and in this area it would seem reasonable to cast the net wide and consider each of the following meanings equally legitimate:

---

[2] See Harrop A. Freeman, "Civil Disobedience," in *Civil Disobedience,* Harrop A. Freeman *et al.* (Santa Barbara, 1966).

1. *The reference can be to a recognition of general obligations of citizenship and thus to the legitimacy of the existing legal order as a whole; pains taken to limit defiance to a particular legal clause or policy, and/or to avoid violence, may* (but need not) *be construed as an affirmation of general citizenship duties.*

2. *"Civil" can be taken to refer to the opposite of "military," in a broad sense. The customary stress on nonviolence may be construed to signify either* (a) *a recognition of the state's claim to monopoly with respect to legitimate use of physical violence, or* (b) *a rejection of all physical violence as illegitimate or morally wrong under all circumstances regardless of purpose.*

3. *"Civil" can refer to the opposite of "uncivil" or "uncivilized"; acts of civil disobedience may seek to embody ideals of citizenship or morality that will inspire adversaries and/or onlookers, hopefully, toward more civilized behavior, or behavior more in harmony with the ideals that inspire a given campaign of civil disobedience.*

4. *"Civil" can also be taken to refer to public as distinct from private: as citizens we act in public. Acts of civil disobedience seek not only to affirm a principle in private, but to call public attention to the view that a principle of moral importance is held to be violated by a law or a policy sanctioned by public authorities.*

5. *"Civil" can suggest that the objective of obedience is to institute changes in the political system, affecting not only one individual's or group's liberties but the liberties of all citizens. A religious sect persisting in outlawed practices of worship* (say, the Peyote cult among western American Indians, before the U.S. Supreme Court came to its rescue) *may insist only on being left alone, or may at the same time consciously assert a principle to the effect that other sects, too, should enjoy the equivalent rights. Degrees of consciousness about the wider implications of disobedient behavior are not well suited as conceptual demarcation lines, however, and it would seem most practical to include even very parochially motivated acts of disobedience within the scope of the concept of civil disobedience.*

The ambiguities of the term "civil" are far from exhausted by this brief list, but the five meanings presented are probably among the more common. The chances are that most of those who practice civil disobedience think of their behavior as "civil" in a sense, whether articulated or not, which embraces more than one of these associations, and perhaps others as well.

Returning now to the definition with which we began, let us note, first, that acts of civil disobedience may be illegal and legal at the same time, in cases of conflict of laws. For example, disobedience campaigns have been conducted against state segregation laws in the American South, in the belief that under the Federal Constitution such acts of disobedience will *eventually* be deemed legal in the Federal courts.

The ends of civil disobedience must be public and limited, it is suggested. The ostensible aim cannot, within the reference proposed, be a private or business advantage; it must have *some* reference to a conception of justice or the common good. (This is not to deny, of course, that individual motives for engaging in civil disobedience at times may be neurotic or narrowly self-seeking, consciously or subconsciously.) The proclaimed ends must be limited, too; they must fall short of seeking the complete abolition of the existing legal system; those who want a "nonviolent revolution" may engage in civil disobedience, but they, too, proclaim specific, limited ends each time. Also, according to the usage recommended here, the proclaimed aims must fall short of intending the physical or moral destruction of adversaries, even if at times a calculable risk of casualties may be tolerated. The ends of civil disobedience must be potentially acceptable to those in the *role* of adversaries even if to current adversaries they may be anathema on psychological grounds.

Above all, the proclaimed ends of civil disobedience, as the concept is understood here, must be formulated with a view to making them appear morally legitimate to onlookers and to the public. Educational objectives prompt most civil disobedience campaigns, and are never wholly absent. If a trade union violates the law to gain equality or justice, in some sense, for their members, we may speak of civil disobedience, but not if a key position in the economic system tempts a union to violate the law for the purpose of extorting unreasonable privileges in return for obeying the law. A civil disobedience campaign can aim at destroying privileges considered unjust, but not at abolishing the right to equal protection of an already underprivileged minority group.

The "carefully chosen and limited means" of civil disobedience are calculated to achieve maximum efficiency in promoting the ends and also maximum economy in seeking to reduce as much as possible the cost of the struggle in terms of suffering and deprivation. True, Gandhi at times stressed the value of bearing or even seeking suffering, but he always wanted to avoid inflicting suffering on his adversaries or on third parties.

"Civil disobedience" should be kept apart from "nonviolent action." The latter concept by definition rules out violent acts while the former does not as defined here.[3] Among some pacifist believers in civil disobedience it seems to be assumed that a complete commitment to nonviolence, even in the sense of avoiding the provocation of violence on the part of adversaries, is ethically superior to a more pragmatic attitude toward the possible use of violence. No such assumption is made here. "Carefully chosen and limited means" in the definition at the outset refers to choice of means rationally calculated to promote the limited ends. For many reasons it seems plausible that such rational calculation normally will suggest strenuous efforts toward either avoidance or reduction of violence. Civil disobedience activists and social scientists ought to be equally interested in research on the causation and consequences of violence and nonviolence under conditions of social conflict; the expansion of this type of knowledge would seem of crucial importance for achieving increasingly realistic calculations of the most effective and economic means toward the chosen ends of civil disobedience campaigns, and also toward determining when such campaigns are and when they are not likely to be successful.[4]

III

My normative position is essentially a simple one, even if it, like any other normative position, raises complex issues in application. Man and his world are, after all, almost infinitely complex.

The primary purpose of politics and of government, I hold, is to protect human life, and to expand the sphere of freedoms securely enjoyed by the individual—all individuals, mind you, on an equal basis. If all are equally entitled to grow and live in freedom, then those currently most deprived, in every unequal society, must have the highest priority claim on protection by the state.

A different way of stating the same fundamental commitment is to say that governmental coercion—and governments are by their nature coercive—can be justified only to the extent that

---

[3] An opposite view is adopted by Hugo A. Bedau, "On Civil Disobedience," *Journal of Philosophy,* LVIII (1961), 653–665; by Carl Cohen, "Essence and Ethics of Civil Disobedience," *The Nation,* CXCVIII (March 16, 1964), 257–262; and by Freeman, *op. cit.*

[4] My discussion in section II is adapted from my article, "Civil Disobedience," in the *International Encyclopedia of the Social Sciences* (1967).

it in fact serves to reduce coercion; and physical violence and oppressive economic deprivation prior to other, less debilitating restraints.

If I may anticipate for a moment my argument in the next section, no political order achieved so far, and that goes for our western ways of government, too, has been justifiable in these terms, if reasonably strictly construed. Demands on government arising from the lesser pains and frustrations suffered by influentials have generally taken precedence over demands arising, or demands that *should* arise, from the more debilitating indignities suffered by the poor and the inarticulate —whose very deprivation (with its cultural and psychological aspects) in fact prevents them, except in exceedingly rare revolutionary situations, almost unthinkable in the privilege-entrenched North American political order, from playing any political role at all.

According to the classical ideals, democracy should be a commonwealth of political equals, who are free to advance the common good and also their own good by constitutional means —that is, by legislation, brought about by processes designed to make sure that the laws express the well-deliberated desires *and* needs of the people. I feel committed to the aim of achieving democracy in this ideal sense because such a system would, to the extent that it could be brought about, be hospitable to respect for life and for human rights on the basis of equality. It would be easy to obey, presumably, the laws enacted in an ideal democracy. I shall argue, however, that this ideal cannot be realized, or even appreciably advanced, without a much expanded role for civil disobedience, given our present political order.

IV

Many leading political theorists would have us believe that western democracy as we know it in the United States and Britain today comes about as close to perfection as can any political order that fallible human beings can hope to attain. Some would have us dismiss as senseless "extremism" any radical questioning of the merits of our political *status quo,* and have even proclaimed an "end of ideology."

The classical ideals of democracy (excepting, most notably, the rule of law) have been all but abandoned by some of these theorists, or at any rate have been restructured so that their commitment to democracy has become a commitment to uphold what essentially amounts to the *status quo*.[5] Now, Bertrand Russell has remarked somewhere that the ruler of Hobbes's state would be far worse than Hobbes himself imagined if the citizens were to be as meek and submissive as Hobbes wanted. It is a fundamental part of my own thesis that every political order tends to become more tyrannical the more submissive its citizens are. Western democracies probably form no exception to this rule. In fact, as de Tocqueville saw, a peculiar hazard of democracies is that citizens are brought not only to comply with authority edicts but to regard them as binding morally as well, since they claim to represent the people's will.[6]

Democratic governments, like all others, seek to isolate and emasculate radical dissenters. If the domestic methods of democratic governments have been less extreme and less brutal than those of most dictator regimes, this probably reflects the usual stability of established democratic regimes, more so than any real appreciation of the value of dissent and dialogue about political fundamentals. True, the right to dissent is proclaimed as one of the many political virtues of our system, so that radical dissenters must be tolerated to a considerable extent, but there are many safeguards against permitting a fair hearing for their views. States and indeed all large organizations, as numerous studies from Michels'[7] on have shown, tend toward oligarchy and toward becoming instruments in the service of their respective oligarchies, at the expense of rank-and-file members.

The fact that the Anglo-Saxon democracies at most times have been able to dispense with the coarser methods of political repression, which in itself should be valued and indeed welcomed as a major achievement of our species, is at the same time a testimonial to the unlikelihood of any real changes taking place within the framework of established democracies. It is argued in our civics texts that the governing political parties in democracies tend to accept defeat at the polls gracefully because they know they may have a chance to come back to power again another time, if the rules of the democratic game are maintained. A fuller explanation of this willingness

[5] See, most notably, the last chapters in each of the following volumes: Bernard R. Berelson, Paul F. Lazarsfeld, and William N. McPhee, *Voting* (Chicago, 1954); Seymour Martin Lipset, *Political Man* (Garden City, 1960); and Gabriel A. Almond and Sidney Verba, *The Civic Culture* (Princeton, 1963).

[6] See Alexis de Tocqueville, *Democracy in America* (New York, 1954), Vintage Books ed., especially Vol. I, Chap. XV.

[7] Robert Michels, *Political Parties* (Glencoe, 1949, 1915).

to abide by election results surely should include, however, especially in the United States but in most other democracies as well, the fact that not much is really at stake in elections, generally speaking, for the major interests. The tradition of "negative government" prior to Franklin Roosevelt made the United States government unable, even if it had been willing, to reduce the amount of socioeconomic injustice; and even after Roosevelt, though a trend toward "positive government" has been growing, and perhaps culminating with the early years of Lyndon Johnson, the division of powers, the conservatism of the mass media, the enormity of the economic power of the privileged strata, and a host of other circumstances have made it virtually impossible to expect government to become an instrument, even in part, for the interests of the downtrodden, or for the enlargement of human rights at the expense of privileges.

True, there have been proclaimed programs of Square Deal, New Freedom, New Deal, Fair Deal, New Frontier, and more recently, the Great Society. In its affluence America has been able to keep most of its underprivileged from actual starvation and has increased the opportunities for gifted or energetic young people of all classes and races. This has been done perhaps in part with lofty motives but probably also in part to attract votes and also, especially in recent decades, out of concern for America's image abroad; surely also in part as a means to forestall or reduce the incidence of acts of desperation like race riots, industrial violence, and the like.

As Dahl has observed, democratic government, even an ideal democratic government, has no ready way of registering the intensity of feeling about public issues.[8] "One man, one vote" means equal weight for the concerned vote and the indifferent vote; for the intelligent and the foolish vote; for the vote in defense of elemental dignities of life and the vote in pursuit of added privileges for groups already favored. As David Truman has observed, however, in our democracy the potential existence of new groups and new coalitions does put some limits on what a government will do, even if elected by a wide margin.[9] But the trouble is, as most of our civic culture-championing pluralists fail to acknowledge, that the potential groups and coalitions a president or governor or mayor needs to worry about are rarely made up of the underprivileged—

---

[8] Robert A. Dahl, *A Preface to Democratic Theory* (Chicago, 1963), Phoenix Books ed., especially pp. 48–50, 90 ff., and 134–135.
[9] David B. Truman, *The Governmental Process* (New York, 1951), *passim*.

except, perhaps, if they are desperate to the point of being riot-prone, or intelligently led to the point of being prone to engage in civil disobedience. Normally, except in countries with strong political labor movements, the underprivileged have been made politically ineffective to the point of emasculation by their circumstances of life; coalitions of influentials and privileged are usually the only effective potential groups, and theirs are the interests that most executives prefer to appease rather than confront. As Murray Edelman puts it, in every conflict of interest between the many and the few, the many tend to be given symbolic gratification by way of democratic rhetoric and nice-sounding laws, while the few are given the tangible benefits, including a way of enforcing or not enforcing the laws that suit them.[10]

As Kolko and others have documented, the structure of economic wealth and power in this country has not been changed at all for the last half-century.[11] For all the slogans, Square Deal to Great Society, political influence remains in the hands of the economically strong while the poor remain inarticulate and largely without influence. Even the trade unions, though in the past they have served the economic interests of some categories of poor, are politically irrelevant today, having become guilds for the protection of their own shrinking number of members only, and uninterested in general issues of social justice, either domestically or internationally.

I am not out to castigate United States democracy as distinct from other democracies. My point is that the realities of western democracies keep stacking the cards in favor of the influentials and the privileged, who are therefore in a position to keep expanding their power and influence, while the underprivileged are becoming less and less able even to *think* and much less to act politically. The United States is merely the society in which this development has come the farthest, perhaps because the accumulation of private wealth has been and is larger than anywhere else. Ironically and significantly, the United States is also the modern nation most explicitly committed to the political principles of democracy, and has been for the longest time.

Democracy as we know it in the West has become, it would seem, an almost foolproof instrumentality to preserve the political and socioeconomic *status quo*. Orderly political change has become impracticable, I submit, except to the extent that

---

[10] Murray Edelman, *The Symbolic Uses of Politics* (Urbana, 1964).
[11] Gabriel Kolko, *Wealth and Power in America* (New York, 1962).

citizens free themselves from their prevailing belief that democracy has already been achieved, and that the laws enacted in their society therefore must be obeyed.

Under conditions of democratic pluralism, an uncritical submission to the rule of law means not only the shunning of violence but also, in effect, the abandonment of all intelligent effort to work effectively for changing the system. For it means agreeing in advance to live by rules in fact operating to forestall the development of democracy in any real sense. These are the rules by which the powerful have become more powerful, and the powerless more emasculated, while only the appearances of democracy have been maintained—an ever more challenging task, incidentally, but a task to which our media of communication and indoctrination so far have proved equal. Thus the discrepancies between our rose-colored perceptions of a government "by the people" and the stark realities of poverty and oppression have kept on growing.

Apparently, stability has kept growing, too. But for the human factors of alienation and desperation, this process might continue indefinitely. But social pathologies were bound to grow below the surface. Not only common crimes but also disorderly attacks against "the system" are likely to occur to an increasing extent. They will be destructive of lives and property but will fail to promote more democratic realities. They may well tempt the present and future American governments to engage in increasingly reckless violence abroad, as a means of seeking to recover national unity, to avoid the alternative of reducing the domestic socioeconomic injustice at the root of national disunity.

V

All organizational leaders are troubled by the fact that, as Philip Selznick has put it, human beings can be recalcitrant rather than pliant instruments in their designs.[12] This goes for statesmen and political leaders as well. Dictators may have to rely on secret police and recurrent terror to prevent revolutions and *coups d'état.* Democratic statesmen in some ways have an easier time of it, as we have seen, as they normally can rely on a broad consensus affirming not only a faith in democracy as an ideal but a belief that democracy has been achieved and that all democratically enacted laws must be obeyed, and that

---

12 Philip Selznick, *TVA and the Grass Roots* (Berkeley, 1949), pp. 252–253.

whatever is done by democratically elected statesmen is legitimate. If Texas oilmen in effect are subsidized by all consumers of gasoline; if wars are fought to install aggressive satellite regimes on unwilling foreign nations; and so on: To the extent that people believe democracy has been achieved in their country they tend to become pliant rather than recalcitrant; they can be "managed."

Yet degrees of and extent of pliancy vary with issues and with events. Generally speaking, it is greater the less immediately the individual is affected by particular laws and policies— or rather, the less he is aware of being affected. A policy of supplying faraway foreign dictators with napalm and other achievements of American know-how for use against their rebellious compatriots is readily accepted as being in the national interest on the say-so of a president; it is only when sons and brothers and boy friends and husbands are sent off to kill and to risk their own lives far away that a policy may be questioned or even resisted.

On the other hand, these are precisely the situations in which strong feelings about the inherently superior righteousness of the "democratic cause" are most easily developed, and an intelligent dialogue made most difficult.[13] At such times public witness by way of disobedient acts may be the only way to convey to the average citizen even an *awareness* of the existence of strongly felt dissent. In times of hero-worship, resistance to jingo sentiments must perhaps be heroically bold in order to become visible, lest the average citizen either remain unaware of the existence of dissent or else confuse opposition to a war with cowardice.

Ironically, the most striking example of bold and also effective resistance to legislation in recent American history had little to do with heroism. I refer to our experiment with Prohibition during the twenties. Let me stress that this is not an example of civil disobedience as defined in this paper, for the Volstead Act was usually evaded in secret, even if Clarence Darrow is said to have referred to bootleggers as fighters for American liberties and to have predicted the erection of statues to Al Capone in many a public park.[14] My point is simply that

---

[13] "The first casualty in every shooting war is common sense, and the second is free and open discussion," wrote James Reston in *The New York Times* of February 12, 1965, five days after the beginning of the United States bombing of North Vietnam.

[14] See Harry Elmer Barnes, *Prohibition Versus Civilization* (New York, 1932), pp. 71–72.

our own recent history testifies to the power of popular defiance to change a law.[15] This result is more likely to come about, presumably, the more widespread and determined the defiance, civil or not, of a particular law.

But there is little prospect, alas, that laws and policies supported by far more powerful economic interests—say the Vietnam war, or the continuing inequities in our school systems—can be changed by way of disobedience, civil or not. It takes knowledge, independence of livelihood, and certain skills in interpersonal relations to engage in civil disobedience. True, something has been and more will perhaps be accomplished in race relations, a field in which some acts of disobedience against some southern state laws have become almost respectable elsewhere in the nation, under the impact of a growing concern for America's image abroad in its confrontation with communist nations. But issues of war and peace are beyond the reach of most people, as are even more the underlying issues of an economic system which depends on preparations for war and serves to bolster and expand privileges instead of rights.

Our only hope, as I see it, is in education—that is, education toward intellectual and political independence for the individual. We badly need an education that enables and encourages each young citizen to think for himself about the proper aims of government, or the state, and to judge by his own standards to what extent the government of his own nation pursues those aims. Only to that extent should it have his support. To the extent that his government pursues illegitimate aims, in his judgment, or employs means subversive of and menacing to the values a just government must uphold, civil disobedience may well be the right response if acts of protest within the framework of existing legislation would be ineffective or take too long a time.[16] Or it may be the wrong response. My point is that a man is not educated to the point of political responsibility unless he can and will make this decision for himself.

And the most elementary requirement of political education, thus conceived, is liberation from the prevailing pluralist demo-

[15] In fact, Mr. Darrow is quoted as claiming that this "nullification," as he calls it, is a traditional American way of changing the law, *ibid*. See also Clarence Darrow and Victor S. Yerros, *The Prohibition Mania* (New York, 1927).

[16] "What I have to do is see, at any rate, that I do not lend myself to the wrong which I condemn. As for adopting the ways which the state has provided for remedying the evil, I know not such ways. They take too much time, and a man's life will be gone." Henry David Thoreau, "Civil Disobedience," in his *Walden and Other Writings* (New York, 1950), Modern Library ed., pp. 644–645.

cratic myth, which claims a reverence for the Majesty of the Law—all laws!—on the ground that they have been democratically enacted. It is about time, I think, that political theorists, at least, free themselves from the stultifying grip of this myth, however convenient it may be as a rationalization for political inaction and, in my terms, political irresponsibility.

VI

In psychological terms, attention to the functions of political opinions for the individual provides an additional ground for arguing that the individual should strive to become sovereign in the choice of his fundamental political commitments.

We are aware today of the wide extent to which government policies as well as public opinion are the outcome of neurotic anxieties and fears, which are difficult to diagnose with exactitude and are more difficult still to cure. Modern psychologists and political scientists have established in a general way how political opinions are developed to meet personality needs, and how the individual's ability to cope with anxieties at various levels determines his capacity for rationality and a realistic long-term assessment of his own good as well as the common good.[17] Most people are neurotic and conformist as well as rational, in varying mixtures; enlightened, civilized policies are unlikely to emanate from democratic processes except to the extent that influential leaders become capable of farsighted rationality. Yet democratic competition for office and power almost invariably strengthens the neurotic aspects and lessens the rational aspects of political behavior; most electoral appeals, especially in times of crises when cool rationality is most needed, are directed to anxieties and paranoid sentiments rather than to reason or enlightened hopes.

The conscientious dissenter who cannot opt out of this system has no easy guide available for determining when to obey and when to disobey the law. There is no general solution to his dilemma, except to urge that he insist on protecting his own sanity and powers of reason, the autonomy of his own social conscience, and his own right to grow toward whatever moral stature or humanity he is capable of achieving. The criteria for concrete decisions to obey or disobey must depend

---

[17] See especially Daniel Katz, "The Functional Approach to the Study of Attitudes," *Public Opinion Quarterly*, XXIV (1960), 163–204; and M. Brewster Smith, Jerome S. Bruner and Robert W. White, *Opinions and Personality* (New York, 1964). In this section, too, several paragraphs are adapted from my forthcoming article for the *International Encyclopedia, op. cit.*

on the nature of each situation, anticipating by careful inquiry and reflection the consequences of either obeying or disobeying; but they must also depend on each moral dissenter's personality and beliefs, especially his beliefs concerning priorities among evils or among good causes.

This open-endedness of the modern dilemma of civil disobedience fits well with Albert Camus's theory of rebellion as an individual responsibility: While only an active and pressing social conscience can bring an individual to full life as a human being, his responsibility for action or inaction as a social being is strictly individual and lonesome. What is given, according to Camus, is only the immorality or inhumanity of a life of acquiescence in evil; he goes even further and argues that a commitment never to resist violence with violence amounts to such acquiescence, or "bourgeois nihilism." But he offers no guidelines for concrete political decisions.[18]

It is worth noting that legislation to legitimize certain grounds for conscientious objection to military service has tended to excuse only those who could prove they had no rational, politically articulate basis for objecting to becoming soldiers. In the United States as in other western democracies, only a religious basis for objection was recognized at the outset. To the extent that the courts or subsequent legislation have attempted to liberalize the rules, as has happened in the States and in other western nations, the tendency has been to lower the demand for evidence of church membership or religious orthodoxy of some kind, but to keep insisting that objection is no longer legitimate unless it remains apolitical, and condemns all past and future warfare indiscriminately.

For contrast, take Bertrand Russell's response when he was once chided on a British "Brain Trust" program over the BBC for having gone to jail for resisting World War I as a pacifist, while he had supported World War II, and now once again seemed prepared to object to the point of civil disobedience against preparations for a third world war. He said, "I want to pick my wars." This, in my view, is a simple but profound statement of responsible citizenship. What other human right can be more basic than the right to choose what cause, if any, to kill for and to die for?

Yet this, of course, is precisely the kind of human right that no government, dictatorial or democratic, wishes to grant. Legal recognition of politically motivated conscientious objection would hamper the pursuit of "tough" foreign policies in a way that religiously or pacifistically motivated objection

---

[18] Albert Camus, *The Rebel* (New York, 1958), especially Part V.

will not. Any government can limit the influence of saints; far more dangerous to established privileges and policies are citizens who combine radical dissent with political know-how, or saintly aims like social justice, freedom, or peace with flexible tactics of protest inside and outside the law.

It seems to me that Camus's theory of rebellion has contributed at least two important thoughts toward a modern theory of civil disobedience. One, which has been touched on already, is his view that a rigid adherence to nonviolent means of protest in some situations may amount to acquiescence in continued violence and oppression. For him as for the orthodox pacifists, violence is always the supreme evil; but to him it is in part an empirical question whether violence in given situations can be overcome or reduced by entirely nonviolent means (or, of course, by any combination of violent and nonviolent means). In my view and in Max Weber's terminology, he argues that an ethics of *a priori* duty must be supplanted by an ethics of responsibility, a responsibility for anticipating as full a range of consequences of alternative means of action as experience and research can establish, if there is time, before deciding on a course of action, nonviolent or in part violent.

It is precisely because the consequences of revolutionary activity are likely to be both violent and to a large extent unpredictable (especially with respect to the extent and duration of acts of violence) that Camus is so strongly in favor of rebellion, in his sense, as an alternative to revolution. His rebel is the piecemeal revolutionary—the politically responsible citizen who is committed to fight violence and oppression by the most *economic* means, i.e., he seeks to avoid the use of violence whenever possible, and above all to avoid the use of remedies that could be worse than the present evil—worse in terms of degrees and extent of violence suffered. With respect to his aims, Camus's rebel is related to the revolutionary in that he will be satisfied with nothing less than complete justice or a complete end to oppression, but he is apt to be less confident that this utopia can ever be fully realized. When it comes to his choice of means, Camus's rebel is identical with the type of responsible citizen extolled in these pages: the person who honors not the Rule of Law so much as the Rule of Justice, and who is prepared to support or commit civil disobedience against oppressive government or legislation.

If Camus has helped draw the demarcation line and develop the rationale for modern civil disobedience, as distinguished from revolutionary activity,[19] he has also, as a second contri-

---

[19] To distinguish the two concepts is not to say that the same person or movement cannot at the same time believe in civil disobedience and in

bution to a modern theory or civil disobedience, been the first to articulate the psychological necessity of being a rebel, or a citizen in principle prepared to commit civil disobedience against oppressive laws and policies, if one is to achieve one's full human stature. Rebellion, as a manifestation of revulsion against injustice, is to Camus an essential dimension of the free man's life; only men who remain too neurotic, too stymied to develop a consciousness of their own humanity, their own solidarity with all men, can remain indifferent and passive when confronted with victims or perpetrators of injustice. In a cruelly competitive society, perhaps most men remain stymied, or in Camus's sense less than fully human; yet at all times there have been rebels, believers in obedience to their own principles as a higher necessity than obedience to the powers that be, or the laws with which these powers guard their interests. I have argued in this chapter that only a good supply of such individuals can help us come closer to the achievement of democracy; Camus argues that only such qualities in a man can help him achieve his own individuality as well as his own humanity.

But in our time, with its unprecedented technology, capable of bureaucratizing acts of murder, and of dehumanizing men who may make decisions about life or death for millions of fellow human beings, the more effective education of an expanding supply of rebels may well be our civilization's last hope of survival. Without thousands of young men able and willing to disobey calls to contribute to moral monstrosities like, for example, American warfare in Vietnam, where is there hope that the bureaucratized, consensus-manufacturing forces of destruction of the modern superpowers—the Leviathans of our time—can be checked before our civilization becomes engulfed in a third world war?

In the name of democracy a new kind of servitude has developed in the West. Witness the hundreds of thousands of men who, educationally unequipped to judge for themselves, have been shipped to a far-off land to kill and perhaps die for what they cheerfully believe is the cause of democracy, or at any rate their own nation's best interests. And witness the many admonitions to dissenters against the war policy that they limit their protests to legal channels, again in the name of democracy, lest its rules of order be violated. Naturally, only

---

revolution. For example, one may have proximate or short-range aims to be served by civil disobedience and yet believe in eventual revolution; or one may believe in revolution as an ultimate resort if results of civil disobedience are too limited or too slow.

harmless, easily manageable forms of protest are desired; violence in contests for power at home is inveighed against with democratic moral fervor by the same leaders who look to violence as almost the only way to engage in contests for power abroad. Advocacy of force and violence at home is condemned, and so is advocacy *against* use of force and violence abroad, for both kinds of advocacy could menace the *status quo.*

Let me conclude by returning to the most fundamental argument of this essay: Governments exist for the purpose of establishing and defending human rights, with the most basic rights, like protection against violence and starvation, taking precedence over less basic rights. The common good, according to this view, hinges on the good of the least favored individuals, taking into account also the prospects for those not yet born.

This or any similar type of basis for political obligation directed to the ends of politics, which relegates not only democracy but also respect for the law in all its alleged majesty to the status of means, takes the vestiges of the role of subject out of the role of citizen. It substitutes an ethics of individual responsibility for the probable results of one's political behavior, including law-abiding as well as legally obligated behavior, for an ethics of duty to subordinate conscience, knowledge, and individual judgment to existing legal norms, government directives, or a majority vote.

The judgments at Nuremberg and the wide attention given to the Eichmann trial in Jerusalem have increased acceptance for the view that the autonomy of the individual conscience is a vital resource in our modern technological and bureaucratized civilization. The "essence of totalitarian government, and perhaps the nature of every bureaucracy," writes Hannah Arendt, "is to make functionaries and mere cogs in the administrative machinery out of men, and thus to dehumanize them."[20] "Each time we obey an order from higher up, without evaluating and judging it in moral terms, there is the Eichmann within ourselves bending his neck," writes a reviewer of Arendt's book, and further observes: "Eichmann was neither intellectually nor morally worse equipped than most people . . . his fault was that he did not feel personally responsible for what his government did. In this respect he is not unique."[21]

[20] *Eichmann in Jerusalem* (New York, 1963), p. 289.

[21] Jens Bjorneboe, "Eichmann i vaare hjerter" ("Eichmann in our hearts"), *Orientering*, Oslo (December 18, 1965).

The human race may never fully achieve democracy; no large nation is likely to come very close to this exacting ideal, although I believe it can be approximated in the foreseeable future in university communities and perhaps in some other local communities. What is important, if we value freedom for all on the basis of justice, is that we move toward rather than away from democracy. For this purpose our educational institutions must try to produce, I submit, men and women less like Eichmann, and more like his opposite, more like Camus's rebel. The rebel, or the believer in civil disobedience in the fight against oppression, is to this writer the model of the responsible citizen who wishes to promote democracy. What we don't need, in my view, and what we are now oversupplied with, is the cheerful, loyal, pliable, law-abiding, basically privatist type of citizen extolled not only in our high school civics texts but in our professional civic culture and end of ideology literature as well.

Mohandas K. Gandhi

Non-violence

My Task

426. In the past, non-co-operation has been deliberately expressed in violence to the evil-doer. I am endeavouring to show to my countrymen that violent non-co-operation only multiplies evil and that as evil can only be sustained by violence, withdrawal of support of evil requires complete abstention from violence. Non-violence implies voluntary submission to the penalty for non-co-operation with evil.—*YI*, 23–3–22, 168.

427. I am not a visionary. I claim to be a practical idealist. The religion of non-violence is not meant merely for the *rishis*[1] and saints. It is meant for the common people as well. Non-violence is the law of our species as violence is the law of the brute. The spirit lies dormant in the brute and he knows no law but that of physical might. The dignity of man requires obedience to a higher law—to the strength of the spirit.

I have therefore ventured to place before India the ancient law of self-sacrifice. For, *satyagraha*[2] and its off-shoots, non-co-operation and civil resistance, are nothing but new names for the law of suffering. The *rishis,* who discovered the law of

These passages are from *Selections from Gandhi,* Second Edition, edited by Professor Nirmal Kumar Bose, Navajivan Publishing House, 1957, pp. 149, 153–154, 156–157, 158–159, 163–167, and 170–172. They are reprinted here by permission of the Navajivan Trust, Copyright © 1957 the Navajivan Trust. The abbreviations at the ends of selections indicate their original sources: *YI-Young India* (1919–32); *Tagore-Young India* (1919–22), published in book form by Tagore and Company (1922); *H*-the *Harijan* (1933 onwards); *Nat.-Speeches and Writings of Mahatma Gandhi,* Fourth Edition, G. A. Natesan and Company; and *IHR-Hind Swaraj or Indian Home Rule,* 1944, Navajivan Publishing House. These brief selections can but give a hint of the richness of Gandhi's thought, and it is hoped that the reader will be stimulated to read more deeply into his writings. Mohandas K. Gandhi (1869–1948) needs little introduction. A truly outstanding religious and moral thinker, he was the leader in India's successful struggle for independence. His personal life was a testimony to the sincerity of his beliefs; and he was the most eloquent, articulate, and convincing spokesman for nonviolence that the world has known.

[1] [Holy Hindu sages, saints, or inspired poets. Ed.]

[2] [This has been variously rendered into English as love-force, truth-force, or soul-force. Ed.]

non-violence in the midst of violence, were greater geniuses than Newton. They were themselves greater warriors than Wellington. Having themselves known the use of arms, they realized their uselessness and taught a weary world that its salvation lay not through violence but through non-violence.—*YI*, 11–8–20, *Tagore*, 712. . . .

Moral Equivalent of War

439. Up to the year 1906, I simply relied on appeal to reason. I was a very industrious reformer. I was a good draftsman, as I always had a close grip of facts which in its turn was the necessary result of my meticulous regard for truth. But I found that reason failed to produce an impression when the critical moment arrived in South Africa. My people were excited; even a worm will and does sometimes turn—and there was talk of wreaking vengeance. I had then to choose between allying myself to violence or finding out some other method of meeting the crisis and stopping the rot and it came to me that we should refuse to obey legislation that was degrading and let them put us in jail if they liked. Thus came into being the moral equivalent of war. I was then a loyalist, because, I implicitly believed that the sum total of the activities of the British Empire was good for India and for humanity. Arriving in England soon after the outbreak of the war I plunged into it and later when I was forced to go to India as a result of the pleurisy that I had developed, I led a recruiting campaign at the risk of my life, and to the horror of some of my friends. The disillusionment came in 1919 after the passage of the Black Rowlatt Act and the refusal of the Government to give the simple elementary redress of proved wrongs that we had asked for. And so, in 1920, I became a rebel. Since then the conviction has been growing upon me, that things of fundamental importance to the people are not secured by reason alone but have to be purchased with their suffering. Suffering is the law of human beings; war is the law of the jungle. But suffering is infinitely more powerful than the law of the jungle for converting the opponent and opening his ears, which are otherwise shut, to the voice of reason. Nobody has probably drawn up more petitions or espoused more forlorn causes than I and I have come to this fundamental conclusion that if you want something really important to be done you must not merely satisfy the reason, you must move the heart also. The appeal of reason is more to the head but the penetration of the heart comes from suffering. It opens up the inner understanding in man. Suffering is the badge of the human race, not the sword.—*YI*, 5–11–31, 341.

The Essence of Non-violence

440. (1) Non-violence is the law of the human race and is infinitely greater than and superior to brute force.

(2) In the last resort it does not avail to those who do not possess a living faith in the God of Love.

(3) Non-violence affords the fullest protection to one's self-respect and sense of honour, but not always to possession of land or movable property, though its habitual practice does prove a better bulwark than the possession of armed men to defend them. Non-violence in the very nature of things is of no assistance in the defence of ill-gotten gains and immoral acts.

(4) Individuals and nations who would practise non-violence must be prepared to sacrifice (nations to the last man) their all except honour. It is therefore inconsistent with the possession of other people's countries, i. e. modern imperialism which is frankly based on force for its defence.

(5) Non-violence is a power which can be wielded equally by all—children, young men and women or grown up people, provided they have a living faith in the God of Love and have therefore equal love for all mankind. When non-violence is accepted as the law of life it must pervade the whole being and not be applied to isolated acts.

(6) It is a profound error to suppose that whilst the law is good enough for individuals it is not for masses of mankind. —*H*, 5–9–36, 236. . . .

Why Then not Kill Those Who Oppress Mankind?

446. No human being is so bad as to be beyond redemption, no human being is so perfect as to warrant his destroying him whom he wrongly considers to be wholly evil.—*YI*, 26–3–31, 49.

447. A *satyagrahi* must never forget the distinction between evil and the evil-doer. He must not harbour ill-will or bitterness against the latter. He may not even employ needlessly offensive language against the evil person, however unrelieved his evil might be. For it is an article of faith with every *satyagrahi* that there is no one so fallen in this world but can be converted by love. A *satyagrahi* will always try to overcome evil by good, anger by love, untruth by truth, *himsa* by *ahimsa*.[3] There is no other way of purging the world of evil.—*YI*, 8–8–29, 263.

---

[3] [*Himsa* is the causing of pain or death from anger or selfishness or with the intention to injure. To refrain from doing this is *ahimsa*. Ed.]

Absence of Hatred

448. I hold myself to be incapable of hating any being on earth. By a long course of prayerful discipline, I have ceased for over forty years to hate anybody. I know this is a big claim. Nevertheless, I make it in all humility. But I can and do hate evil wherever it exists. I hate the system of government that the British people have set up in India. I hate the ruthless exploitation of India even as I hate from the bottom of my heart the hideous system of untouchability for which millions of Hindus have made themselves responsible. But I do not hate the domineering Englishmen as I refuse to hate the domineering Hindus. I seek to reform them in all the loving ways that are open to me. My non-co-operation has its roots not in hatred, but in love. My personal religion peremptorily forbids me to hate anybody.—*YI,* 6–8–25, 272.

449. We can only win over the opponent by love, never by hate. Hate is the subtlest form of violence. We cannot be really non-violent and yet have hate in us.—*H,* 17–8–34, 212. . . .

Non-violent Resistance

457. My goal is friendship with the whole world and I can combine the greatest love with the greatest opposition to wrong.—*YI,* 10–3–20, *Tagore,* 139.

458. Non-violence is 'not a resignation from all real fighting against wickedness.' On the contrary, the non-violence of my conception is a more active and real fight against wickedness than retaliation whose very nature is to increase wickedness. I contemplate, a mental and therefore a moral opposition to immoralities. I seek entirely to blunt the edge of the tyrant's sword, not by putting up against it a sharper-edged weapon, but by disappointing his expectation that I would be offering physical resistance. The resistance of the soul that I should offer would elude him. It would at first dazzle him and at last compel recognition from him, which recognition would not humiliate him but would uplift him. It may be urged that this is an ideal state. And so it is.—*YI,* 8–10–25, 346. *cf.* 133, 386, 426, 551. . . .

Limitations of Violence

478. Hitherto I have given historical instances of bloodless non-co-operation. I will not insult the intelligence of the reader

by citing historical instances of non-co-operation combined with violence, but I am free to confess that there are on record as many successes as failures in violent non-co-operation.— *YI*, 4–8–20, *Tagore*, 320.

479. Revolutionary crime is intended to exert pressure. But it is the insane pressure of anger and ill-will. I contend that non-violent acts exert pressure far more effective than violent acts, for that pressure comes from goodwill and gentleness.— *YI*, 26–12–24, 420.

480. I do not blame the British. If we were weak in numbers as they are, we too would perhaps have resorted to the same methods as they are now employing. Terrorism and deception are weapons not of the strong but of the weak. The British are weak in numbers, we are weak in spite of our numbers. The result is that each is dragging the other down. It is common experience that Englishmen lose in character after residence in India and that Indians lose in courage and manliness by contact with Englishmen. This process of weakening is good neither for us two nations, nor for the world.—*YI*, 22–9–20, *Tagore*, 1092.

481. I object to violence because when it appears to do good, the good is only temporary; the evil it does is permanent. I do not believe that the killing of even every Englishman can do the slightest good to India. The millions will be just as badly off as they are today, if someone made it possible to kill off every Englishman tomorrow. The responsibility is more ours than that of the English for the present state of things. The English will be powerless to do evil if we will but be good. Hence my incessant emphasis on reform from within.—*YI*, 21–5–25, 178.

482. Good brought through force destroyed individuality. Only when the change was effected through the persuasive power of non-violent non-co-operation, i.e. love, could the foundation of individuality be preserved, and real, abiding progress be assured for the world.—*H*, 9–3–47, 58.

483. History teaches one that those who have, no doubt with honest motives, ousted the greedy by using brute force against them, have in their turn become a prey to the disease of the conquered.—*YI*, 6–5–26, 164.

To the Revolutionary

484. Those whom you seek to depose are better armed and infinitely better organized than you are. You may not care for your own lives, but you dare not disregard those of your coun-

trymen who have no desire to die a martyr's death.—*YI,* 25–12–24, 428.

485. From violence done to the foreign ruler, violence to our own people whom we may consider to be obstructing the country's progress is an easy natural step. Whatever may have been the result of violent activities in other countries and without reference to the philosophy of non-violence, it does not require much intellectual effort to see that if we resort to violence for ridding society of the many abuses which impede our progress, we shall add to our difficulties and postpone the day of freedom. The people unprepared for reform because unconvinced of their necessity will be maddened with rage over their coercion, and will seek the assistance of the foreigner in order to retaliate. Has not this been happening before our eyes for the past many years of which we have still painfully vivid recollections?—*YI,* 2–1–30, 4.

486. I hold that the world is sick of armed rebellions. I hold too that whatever may be true of other countries, a bloody revolution will not succeed in India. The masses will not respond. A movement in which masses have no active part can do no good to them. A successful bloody revolution can only mean further misery for the masses. For it would be still foreign rule for them. The non-violence I teach is active non-violence of the strongest. But the weakest can partake in it without becoming weaker. They can only be the stronger for having been in it. The masses are far bolder today than they ever were. A non-violent struggle necessarily involves construction on a mass scale. It cannot therefore lead to *tamas*[4] or darkness or inertia. It means a quickening of the national life. That movement is still going on silently, almost imperceptibly, but none the less surely.

I do not deny the revolutionary's heroism and sacrifice. But heroism and sacrifice in a bad cause are so much waste of splendid energy and hurt the good cause by drawing away attention from it by the glamour of the misused heroism and sacrifice in a bad cause.

I am not ashamed to stand erect before the heroic and self-sacrificing revolutionary because I am able to pit an equal measure of non-violent men's heroism and sacrifice untarnished by the blood of the innocent. Self-sacrifice of one innocent man is a million times more potent than the sacrifice of

---

[4] [The darkness, inertia, or dullness that constitutes one of the three primal qualities or elements of matter according to Sankhya philosophy. Ed.]

million men who die in the act of killing others. The willing
sacrifice of the innocent is the most powerful retort to insolent
tyranny that has yet been conceived by God or man.—*YI,*
12–2–25, 60.

Non-violence the Swifter Way

487. The spiritual weapon of self-purification, intangible as it
seems, is the most potent means of revolutionizing one's en-
vironment and loosening external shackles. It works subtly
and invisibly; it is an intense process though it might often
seem a weary and long-drawn process, it is the straightest way
to liberation, the surest and quickest and no effort can be too
great for it. What it requires is faith—an unshakable mountain-
like faith that flinches from nothing.

488. You need not be afraid that the method of non-violence
is a slow long-drawn out process. It is the swiftest the world
has seen, for it is the surest.—*YI,* 30–4–25, 153.

489. India's freedom is assured if she has patience. That
way will be found to be the shortest even though it may appear
to be the longest to our impatient nature. The way of peace in-
sures internal growth and stability.—*YI,* 20–5–26, 184.

Non-violence Also the Nobler Way

490. I am more concerned in preventing the brutalization of
human nature than in the prevention of the sufferings of my own
people. I know that people who voluntarily undergo a course
of suffering raise themselves and the whole of humanity; but
I also know that people who become brutalized in their desperate efforts to get victory over their opponents or to exploit
weaker nations or weaker men, not only drag down themselves
but mankind also. And it cannot be a matter of pleasure to me
or anyone else to see human nature dragged to the mire. If we
are all sons of the same God and partake of the same divine
essence, we must partake of the sin of every person whether
he belongs to us or to another race. You can understand how
repugnant it must be to invoke the beast in any human being,
how much more so in Englishmen, among whom I count numerous friends. I invite you all to give all the help that you can
in the endeavour that I am making.—*YI,* 29–10–31, 325.

491. The doctrine of violence has reference only to the doing of injury by one to another. Suffering injury in one's own
person is on the contrary of the essence of non-violence and
is the chosen substitute for violence to others. It is not because

I value life low that I can countenance with joy thousands voluntarily losing their lives for *satyagraha,* but because I know that it results in the long run in the least loss of life and what is more, it ennobles those who lose their lives and morally enriches the world for their sacrifice.—*YI,* 8–10–25, 345.

492. The method of passive resistance is the clearest and safest, because, if the cause is not true, it is the resisters, and they alone, who suffer.—*Nat.* 305.

493. Passive resistance is an all-sided sword; it can be used anyhow; it blesses him who uses it and him against whom it is used.—*IHR,* 48.

494. The beauty of *satyagraha,* of which non-co-operation is but a chapter, is that it is available to either side in a fight; that it has checks that automatically work for the vindication of truth and justice for that side, whichever it may be, that has truth and justice in preponderating measure. It is as powerful and faithful a weapon in the hand of the capitalist as in that of the labourer. It is as powerful in the hands of the government, as in that of the people, and will bring victory to the government, if people are misguided or unjust, at it will win the battle for the people if the government be in the wrong. Quick disorganization and defeat are bound to be the fate of bolstered up cases and artificial agitations, if the battle is fought with *satyagraha* weapons. Suppose the people are unfit to rule themselves, or are unwilling to sacrifice for a cause, then, no amount of noise will bring them victory in non-co-operation. —*YI,* 23–6–20, *Tagore,* 42. . . .

Can Aggression Be Stopped by Non-violence?

498. *Q.* How could a disarmed neutral country allow other nations to be destroyed? But for our army which was waiting ready at our frontier during the last war we should have been ruined.

A. At the risk of being considered a visionary or a fool I must answer this question in the only manner I know. It would be cowardly of a neutral country to allow an army to devastate a neighbouring country. But there are two ways in common between soldiers of war and soldiers of non-violence, and if I had been a citizen of Switzerland and a President of the Federal State what I would have done would be to refuse passage to the invading army by refusing all supplies. Secondly, by re-enacting a Thermopylae in Switzerland, you would have presented a living wall of men and women and children and invited the invaders to walk over your corpses. You may say that such a thing is beyond human experience and endurance. I say that it is not so. It was quite possible. Last year in Gujarat, women stood *lathi*[5] charges unflinchingly and in Peshawar thousands stood hails of bullets without resorting to violence. Imagine these men and women staying in front of an army requiring a safe passage to another country. The army would be brutal enough to walk over them, you might say. I would then say you will still have done your duty by allowing yourselves to be annihilated. An army that dares to pass over the corpses of innocent men and women would not be able to repeat that experiment. You may, if you wish, refuse to believe in such courage on the part of the masses of men and women; but then you would have to admit that non-violence is made of sterner stuff. It was never conceived as a weapon of the weak, but of the stoutest hearts.

Q. Is it open to a soldier to fire in the air and avoid violence?

A. A soldier who having enlisted himself flattered himself that he was avoiding violence by shooting in the air did no credit to his courage or to his creed of non-violence. In my scheme of things, such a man would be held guilty of untruth and cowardice both—cowardice in that in order to escape punishment he enlisted, and untruth in that he enlisted to serve as soldier and did not fire as expected. Such a thing discredits the cause of waging war against war. The war-resisters have to be like Caesar's wife—above suspicion. Their strength lies in absolute adherence to the morality of the question.—*YI*, 31–12–31, 427.

499. Indeed the weakest State can render itself immune from attack if it learns the art of non-violence. But a small State, no matter how powerfully armed it is, cannot exist in the midst of a powerful combination of well-armed States. It has to be absorbed by or be under the protection of one of the members of such a combination.—*H*, 7–10–39, 293.

500. Whatever Hitler may ultimately prove to be, we know what Hitlerism has come to mean. It means naked, ruthless force reduced to an exact science and worked with scientific precision. In its effect it becomes almost irresistible.

Hitlerism will never be defeated by counter-Hitlerism. It can only breed superior Hitlerism raised to n^{th} degree. What is going on before your eyes is the demonstration of the futility of violence as also of Hitlerism.

What will Hitler do with his victory? Can he digest so much

---

[5] [A weapon used by police for riot control. Ed.]

power? Personally he will go as empty-handed as his not very remote predecessor Alexander. For the Germans he will have left not the pleasure of owning a mighty empire but the burden of sustaining its crushing weight. For they will not be able to hold all the conquered nations in perpetual subjection. And I doubt if the Germans of future generations will entertain unadulterated pride in the deeds fo which Hitlerism will be deemed responsible. They will honour Herr Hitler as a genius, as a brave man, a matchless organizer and much more. But I should hope that the Germans of the future will have learnt the art of discrimination even about their heroes. Anyway I think it will be allowed that all the blood that has been spilled by Hitler has added not a millionth part of an inch to the world's moral stature.

As against this imagine the state of Europe today if the Czechs, the Poles, the Norwegians, the French and the English had all said to Hitler: 'You need not make your scientific preparation for destruction. We will meet your violence with non-violence. You will therefore be able to destroy our non-violent army without tanks, battleships and airships.' It may be retorted that the only difference would be that Hitler would have got without fighting what he has gained after a bloody fight. Exactly. The history of Europe would then have been written differently. Possession might (but only might) have been taken under non-violent resistance, as it has been taken now after perpetration of untold barbarities. Under non-violence, only those would have been killed who had trained themselves to be killed, if need be, but without killing anyone and without bearing malice towards anybody. I dare say that in that case Europe would have added several inches to its moral stature. And in the end I expect it is moral worth that will count. All else is dross.—*H, 22–6–40, 172.*

Howard Zinn

A Fallacy on Law and Order: That Civil Disobedience Must Be Absolutely Nonviolent

Mr. Fortas reminds us that Gandhi, Martin Luther King, and Thoreau, did not believe in violence. He then says: "This is civil disobedience in a great tradition. It is peaceful, nonviolent disobedience of laws which are themselves unjust and which the protester challenges as invalid and unconstitutional." I deal elsewhere in this essay[1] with the other conditions he imposes; here I will concentrate on "peaceful, nonviolent . . ." If Fortas wants to define civil disobedience as having this limitation, this is his right. But others need not accept his definition, and indeed have not.

I would define civil disobedience more broadly, as "the deliberate violation of law for a vital social purpose." Unlike Fortas' definition, this would include violating laws which are immoral whether constitutional or not, and laws which themselves are not at issue as well as those that are. It would leave open the question of the *means* of disobedience, but with two

From *Disobedience and Democracy* by Howard Zinn. Copyright © 1968 by Howard Zinn. Reprinted by permission of Random House, Inc. Additional territory rights granted by Sterling Lord Agency. Zinn's book (subtitled *Nine Fallacies on Law and Order*) is structured as a reply to Abe Fortas' *Concerning Dissent and Civil Disobedience*. Fortas is primarily concerned to claim the following: (1) citizens have an obligation to obey laws even when they disapprove of them; (2) legal channels for the redress of grievances in America are sufficiently adequate to undercut present-day justifications for civil disobedience; and (3) under no circumstances is violence justified in civil disobedience. No selection from Fortas has been included here because other essays in the collection argue for these same points: Rawls (1), Hook (1, 2, and 3), and Gandhi (3). Quotations from *Concerning Dissent and Civil Disobedience* by Abe Fortas © 1968 by Abe Fortas. Reprinted by arrangement with the New American Library, Inc., New York. Howard Zinn is Professor of Government at Boston University. His many publications include the following books: *SNCC, The New Abolitionists* (1964), *Vietnam: The Logic of Withdrawal* (1967), and *The Politics of History* (1970).

[1] [See pp. 8–26 and pp. 32–38 of *Disobedience and Democracy*. Ed.]

thoughts in mind: 1. that one of the moral principles guiding the advocate of civil disobedience is his belief that a nonviolent world is one of his ends, and that nonviolence is more desirable than violence as a means; 2. that in the inevitable tension accompanying the transition from a violent world to a nonviolent one, the choice of means will almost never be pure, and will involve such complexities that the simple distinction between violence and nonviolence does not suffice as a guide.

Such a broader definition has strong support among those who have theorized about civil disobedience, as well as those who have engaged in it. The political philosopher Christian Bay, commissioned to write the article on Civil Disobedience for the *International Encyclopedia of the Social Sciences,* has written: " 'Civil disobedience' should be kept apart from 'nonviolent action.' The latter concept by definition rules out violent acts while the former does not, as defined here." Bay does believe that "carefully chosen and limited means" should be part of the definition of civil disobedience but insists that the key to means is "increasingly realistic calculations of the most effective and economic means toward the chosen ends of civil disobedience campaigns."

Albert Camus spoke in *The Rebel* of the absurdities in which we are trapped, where the very acts with which we seek to do good cannot escape the imperfections of the world we are trying to change. And so the rebel's "only virtue will lie in never yielding to the impulse to allow himself to be engulfed in the shadows that surround him, and in obstinately dragging the chains of evil, with which he is bound, toward the light of good." In this situation, he recognizes that at certain times, for certain reasons, some departure from absolute nonviolence may be necessary. Camus says the rebel must somehow find his solutions along a spectrum of means between two impossible borders:

Absolute non-violence is the negative basis of slavery and its acts of violence; systematic violence positively destroys the living community and the existence we receive from it. To be fruitful, these two ideas must establish final limits.

The abolitionists in pre-Civil War America, although dominated by nonviolent spokesmen like Garrison, also included advocates of violent deeds. Before 1850, the use of violence was confined mostly to the victims of slavery themselves in various insurrections. After 1850, white abolitionists, beginning to think that perhaps slavery could not be dislodged by peaceful methods, looked more favorably on statements like that of Frederick Douglass, writing June 2, 1854, in *Frederick Douglass' Paper:* "Every slavehunter who meets a bloody death in his infernal business is an argument in favor of the manhood of our race."

Fortas points to Thoreau, accurately, as a believer in nonviolence. Yet, when John Brown carried out his attempt to seize arms and instigate a slave rebellion, Thoreau defended him, in "A Plea for Captain John Brown," delivered in Concord and Boston a month before the execution:

'Served him right'—'A dangerous man'—'He is undoubtedly insane.' So they proceed to live their sane, and wise, and altogether admirable lives. . . . It was Brown's peculiar doctrine that a man has a perfect right to interfere by force with the slaveholder, in order to rescue the slave. I agree with him. . . .

Emerson agreed too, speaking of John Brown in Salem; "All gentlemen, of course, are on his side."

Gandhi himself wrote at certain times (1919 and 1921) in *Young India:* "No rules can tell us how this disobedience may be done and by whom, when and where, nor can they tell us which laws foster untruth. It is only experience that can guide us. . . ." And: "I do believe that where there is only a choice between cowardice and violence I would advise violence." This is not to deny that Gandhi was preeminently a believer in nonviolence, but to emphasize that his belief was based on the specific conditions of India in his time, and his emphasis was on pragmatism—letting circumstances and results determine tactics.

Certainly Reinhold Niebuhr interprets Gandhi this way in *Moral Man and Immoral Society,* and while himself advocating nonviolence for the Negro (this was the 1930's) as a practical matter, says:

The differences between violent and non-violent methods of coercion and resistance are not so absolute that it would be possible to regard violence as a morally impossible instrument of social change. . . . The advantages of non-violent methods are very great but they must be pragmatically considered in the light of circumstances.

My point in all this is not at all to establish a case for violence. To me one of the cardinal principles in any moral code is the reduction and elimination of violence. The burden of proof in any argument about social tactics should rest on that person who wants to stray from nonviolence. What I have tried to show is that the problem of tactics in civil disobedience is far more complicated than Mr. Fortas leads us to believe with his easy and righteous dismissal of violence.

What is required is that a set of distinctions be made which will enable us to be more precise in evaluating the problem of violence and nonviolence in civil disobedience. If Mr. Fortas wants to say that civil disobedience must limit itself to non-violent activity, then he is required to explain the moral principles which say why this should be so. This he does not do; he merely asserts his position.

One soon begins to see why he stays away from a careful discussion. When we attempt to put together a set of principles on violence from the scattered remarks in his essay, contradictions and simplifications appear.

For instance, we might conclude from Mr. Fortas' absolute insistence on nonviolence and civil disobedience that it requires no explanation because in his view nonviolence is an ultimate value, *the* supreme value, and therefore self-justifying. But if this were Mr. Fortas' belief, we would expect him to oppose violence in all forms, all the time. We know this is not his credo, because, as we shall see later in more detail, he defends the massive violence of a number of wars.

If some violence is acceptable and other violence is not, then we must have "a principle, a code, a theory" to give us the grounds, to tell us why it is sometimes justifiable in international relations (as by the United States in Korea and Vietnam, according to Mr. Fortas), and never justifiable by groups within a nation (let us say, to cite actions Mr. Fortas is against: burners of draft cards, or breakers of windows at the Pentagon). But Mr. Fortas gives us no such guide.

Let us try to find some principle on which he could possibly justify his absolute prohibition of violence in civil disobedience and his rather easy support of it in international affairs. Perhaps *the importance of the issue* at stake might be one test. There is good reason (as I pointed out earlier, citing Bay, Camus, Niebuhr, Douglass, Thoreau, Gandhi) for not being absolutist in adhering to nonviolence. There are other human values besides peace—so that it is possible to conceive of situations where a disturbance of the peace is justifiable if it results in some massive improvement of the human condition for large numbers of people.

Indeed, Mr. Fortas seems to invoke such a principle when he speaks of the Korean War:

It cost us over 150,000 casualties. [It cost the Koreans a million casualties.] It took us more than three years. But I think it is fairly universal opinion in the Western world that the war was a necessary action; that if we had not taken on the sad and heavy burden of repelling the invasion of South Korea, no one else would or could have done so; and that the consequences of our default would have been greatly to increase the peril to the non-Communist nations of the world—including ourselves.

But if Mr. Fortas justifies violence in Korea because he believes a vital issue was at stake, he cannot with any logical consistency rule out the possibility that for some aggrieved groups in the United States, *some* issues might be important enough to justify some degree of violence.

This brings us to another necessary element of any moral code on violence and nonviolence. Would not any reasonable code have to weigh the *degree* of violence used in any case against the *importance* of the issue at stake? Thus, a massive amount of violence for a small or dubious reason would be harder to justify than a small amount of violence for an important and a clear reason.

We can see now why Fortas might not want to discuss any test by which one could rationally, if roughly, decide when violence might be justified. That would show him supporting the enormous violence of the Korean war for rather hazy international objectives: Was the situation in Korea, North or South, any better because the war was fought? Was the situation in Asia as a whole improved? Did Korea "show" the Communists that they must not seek to unify divided nations by force? Yet we find him opposing any departure from nonviolence connected with removing an obvious, gross injustice, the plight of the black person in America.

One of the reasons Mr. Fortas can get away with his easy dismissal of violence in civil disobedience is that the term "violence," if undefined, can mean anything the reader conjures up in his mind, from breaking a window to dropping a bomb. If he got more specific, and set up a standard which took *degrees* of violence into account, wars might be much harder to justify than local acts of civil disobedience.

There is another point which he slides over—one which is very important, I believe, in drawing up a set of principles on violence and nonviolence in civil disobedience. That is the distinction between violence to people and violence to things; destruction of life, or destruction of property. Mr. Fortas lumps them together as if they were equally reprehensible. He says in his concluding section: "Violence must not be tolerated; damage to persons or property is intolerable." He does not differentiate, in this general prohibition. Yet, once Mr. Fortas has opened the door to *any* distinction on the problem of violence (which he does, once he allows the violence of war), he should not fail to discriminate between people and things. Surely that is one of the cardinal rules in any humanistic philosophy. A fixed devotion to property as something holy, when carried to its extreme, leads policemen to shoot to death black people who are taking *things* from stores.

At one point, Mr. Fortas mentions as intolerable "breaking windows in the Pentagon." Surely that is a mild form of violence compared to the violence a window-breaker might be protesting against—the decisions made in the Pentagon which result in thousands of American men returning to their families in coffins. Should property be so sacred that it must not be despoiled even where there is a need to protest mass murder? Or to express outrage at some great injustice? Should that act of violence in which several Baltimore clergymen burned some draft board records to protest killing in Vietnam be declared wrong, while the act of soldiers burning a peasant village (to see what this means, read Jonathan Schell's book, *The Village of Ben Suc*) is not?

Can we conceive that it might be necessary on certain occasions to depreciate, despoil, occupy or appropriate some piece of property to call attention to some grievous evil—as a wife might find it necessary on occasion to break a dish in anger to awaken her husband to the fact that her rights have been violated? In any case, isn't this distinction between property rights and human rights important in considering whether civil disobedience must always be nonviolent?

Fortas says: "An organized society cannot and will not long endure personal and property damage, whatever the reason, context, or occasion." If he can find a reason, context, occasion to justify 150,000 dead Americans and 1,000,000 dead Koreans, can he find no occasion for "property damage" as a protest by people desperately poor or viciously maltreated or facing arbitrary dispatch to an immoral war?

A carefully drawn moral code on violence in civil disobedience should also consider whether the disorder or violence is controlled or indiscriminate. Crowds rampaging through a city may or may not have a useful effect in changing a situation, but that is not civil disobedience, which involves the deliberate, organized use of power. Violence, no matter how important the cause, becomes unpardonable the more it becomes indiscriminate; hence war, even for "good" reasons, is very hard to justify in these days of high-level bombing and long-range artillery.

Violence might be justifiable as it approaches the focusing and control of surgery. Self-defense is by its nature focused, because it is counterviolence directed only at a perpetrator of violence. (Of course, it has been defined so loosely as to allow all sorts of aggressive actions.) Planned acts of violence in an enormously important cause (the Resistance against Hitler may be an example) could be justifiable. Revolutionary warfare, the more it is aimed carefully at either a foreign controlling power, or a local tyrannical elite, may be morally defensible.

All this is to suggest what criteria need to be kept in mind whenever civil disobedience, in situations of urgency where very vital issues are at stake, and other means have been exhausted, may move from mild actions, to disorder, to overt violence: it would have to be guarded, limited, aimed carefully at the source of injustice, and preferably directed against property rather than people.

There are two reasons for such criteria. One is the moral reason: that violence is in itself an evil, and so can only be justified in those circumstances where it is a last resort in eliminating a greater evil, or in self-defense. The other is the reason of effectiveness: The purpose of civil disobedience is to communicate to others, and indiscriminate violence turns people (rightly) away.

Another point seems so self-evident that Jefferson called it just that in the Declaration of Independence: the idea that all men are created equal. This means that violence to any man must be equated with violence to any other. I say it is self-evident, but we do not act as if it is. We do not react the same to the headline "200 Communists killed today" as we react to "200 Americans killed today." We don't react the same way to 5000 dying in an earthquake in Peru, as to five killed in an auto crash downtown. There are "in" people and "out" people in our normal equations, and they are *not* equal. This is important in considering rules for disorder in civil disobedience; to be aware of this guards against the "natural" reaction—that an egg thrown at one American by another becomes more outrageous than a bomb dropped on Vietnamese.

Likewise, there is a "here" and "there," with no equality between them. It helps explain why the President of the United States may express outrage at a disorderly act of civil disobedience at home, and say nothing about some large act of terror abroad. If it is happening to *them,* we consider the disorder more reasonable than if it is happening to us. At home, this is shown in the fact that the death of blacks is not as disturbing to white Americans as the death of whites, that *actual* destruction in the ghetto is much more tolerable than the *thought* of destruction in the suburbs. The disorder of civil disobedience, because it is directed at our own officials, or our own institutions, therefore is far less tolerated than a much greater disorder, directed at others. But we should insist on the principle that all victims are created equal.

There is an argument for excluding violence from civil disobedience which Justice Fortas does make: that it is impractical; it is not effective in achieving its ends. "But widespread violence—whether it is civil disobedience, or street riots, or guerrilla warfare—will, I am persuaded, lead to repression." He makes this argument specifically with regard to the Negro, saying: "The Negroes have gained much by the strength of their protests and the massiveness of their demonstrations. Even their riots—much as we dislike acknowledging it—produced some satisfaction of their demands. . . . But the reaction to repeated acts of violence may be repression instead of remedy."

By Fortas' own admission, he cannot clearly prove his case for the practicality of nonviolence by the Negro in the United States ("riots . . . produced some satisfaction," he says; and while the result "may" be repression, this is not certain). The evidence so far is that nonviolent tactics have only produced marginal benefits for America's 20 million black people. If there is uncertainty about the practicality of nonviolence in the one example Fortas does give—the race issue—how is he justified in making nonviolence an absolute condition for civil disobedience on *all* issues?

The historical evidence is far from supporting the idea that violence is not effective in producing change. True, there are many instances when violence is completely ineffective, and does result only in repression. But there are other instances when it does seem to bring results. Shays' armed uprising of 1786 had direct effect on tax reform in the Pennsylvania legislature, but more important, an influence on the Constitutional Convention which we cannot begin to measure. Violent labor struggles of the 1930's brought significant gains for labor. Not until Negro demonstrations resulted in violence did the national government begin to work seriously on civil rights legislation. No public statement on the race question has had as much impact as the Kerner Commission report, the direct result of outbreaks of violence in the ghettos.

Barrington Moore's elaborate study of modern social change (*Social Origins of Dictatorship and Democracy*) concludes that violence is an important factor in change. He points out that presumably "peaceful" transitions to modernism, as in England and the United States, really involved large amounts of violence. Certainly this country has not progressed purely on the basis of nonviolent constitutional development. We do not know what effect John Brown's violence had in that complex of events leading to the end of slavery, but it is certainly an open question. Independence, emancipation, labor unions—these basic elements in the development of American democracy all involved violent actions by aggrieved persons.

My point is not that violence is unquestionably an effective method of reforming a society; it seems to me we would have to be extremely careful in adapting historical experience to the conditions of the United States. Each situation in the world is unique and requires unique combinations of tactics. I insist only that the question is so open, so complex, that it would be foolish to rule out at the start, for all times and conditions, all of the vast range of possible tactics beyond strict nonviolence.

Mr. Fortas has given us grounds neither for the immorality, nor for the impracticality of violence in civil disobedience. What remains then to say which is so commonly conceded that it can be a basis for excluding violence absolutely as a form of civil disobedience? Only that it is illegal. We are back to our starting point—Fortas as a Legalist.

The argument of legality, however, is bound to get Mr. Fortas into difficulty—because he does support wars even when they involve violations of international law. He has been, it is known, a close adviser to President Johnson in the conduct of the Vietnam war, which has involved violating the U.N. Charter, the SEATO Treaty, the Kellogg-Briand Pact, and other treaties, all of which, by the U.S. Constitution, are "the highest law of the land." . . .[2]

However, there is no international body to punish the United States for its large act of civil disobedience. Is illegal violence then permissible when it is done by a great power, impervious to retaliation—and impermissible when done by vulnerable dissenters inside that nation? This would not be a moral code but an assertion of realpolitik—might makes right. If this (the legal argument) is behind Fortas' apparent inconsistency on violence, it has not carried us any closer to what he promised: "a principle, a code, a theory" to guide our actions.

[2] [See pp. 68–87 of *Disobedience and Democracy*. Ed.]

Ronald Dworkin

On not Prosecuting Civil Disobedience

How should the government deal with those who disobey the draft laws out of conscience? Many people think the answer is obvious: The government must prosecute the dissenters, and if they are convicted it must punish them. Some people reach this conclusion easily, because they hold the mindless view that conscientious disobedience is the same as lawlessness. They think that the dissenters are anarchists who must be punished before their corruption spreads. Many lawyers and intellectuals come to the same conclusion, however, on what looks like a more sophisticated argument. They recognize that disobedience to law may be *morally* justified, but they insist that it cannot be *legally* justified, and they think that it follows from this truism that the law must be enforced. Erwin Griswold, the Solicitor General of the United States, and the former Dean of the Harvard Law School, appears to have adopted this view in a recent statement. "[It] is of the essence of law," he said, "that it is equally applied to all, that it binds all alike, irrespective of personal motive. For this reason, one who contemplates civil disobedience out of moral conviction should not be surprised and must not be bitter if a criminal conviction ensues. And he must accept the fact that organized society cannot endure on any other basis."

The New York Times applauded that statement. A thousand faculty members of several universities had signed a *Times* advertisement calling on the Justice Department to quash the indictments of the Rev. William Sloane Coffin, Dr. Benjamin Spock, Marcus Raskin, Mitchell Goodman, and Michael Ferber, for conspiring to counsel various draft offenses. The *Times* said that the request to quash the indictments "confused moral rights with legal responsibilities."

Reprinted with permission from *The New York Review of Books*. Copyright © 1968 The New York Review. Ronald Dworkin is Professor of Jurisprudence in the University of Oxford and a Fellow of University College. He was formerly Professor of Law and Master of Trumbull College at Yale. His publications include "Lord Devlin and the Enforcement of Morals" (*Yale Law Journal*, 76[1966], 986–1005) and "The Model of Rules" (*University of Chicago Law Review*, 35[1967], 14–46).

But the argument that, because the government believes a man has committed a crime, it must prosecute him is much weaker than it seems. Society "cannot endure" if it tolerates all disobedience; it does not follow, however, nor is there evidence, that it will collapse if it tolerates some. In the United States prosecutors have discretion whether to enforce criminal laws in particular cases. A prosecutor may properly decide not to press charges if the lawbreaker is young, or inexperienced, or the sole support of a family, or is repentant, or turns state's evidence, or if the law is unpopular or unworkable or generally disobeyed, or if the courts are clogged with more important cases, or for dozens of other reasons. This discretion is not license—we expect prosecutors to have good reasons for exercising it—but there are, at least *prima facie,* some good reasons for not prosecuting those who disobey the draft laws out of conscience. One is the obvious reason that they act out of better motives than those who break the law out of greed or a desire to subvert government. If motive can count in distinguishing between thieves, then why not in distinguishing between draft offenders? Another is the practical reason that our society suffers a loss if it punishes a group that includes—as the group of draft dissenters does—some of its most loyal and law-respecting citizens. Jailing such men solidifies their alienation from society, and alienates many like them who are deterred by the threat. If practical consequences like these argued for not enforcing prohibition, why do they not argue for tolerating offenses of conscience?

Those who think that conscientious draft offenders should always be punished must show that these are not good reasons for exercising discretion, or they must find contrary reasons that outweigh them. What arguments might they produce? There are practical reasons for enforcing draft laws, and I shall consider some of these later. But Dean Griswold and those who agree with him seem to rely on a fundamental moral argument that it would be unfair, not merely impractical, to let the dissenters go unpunished. They think it would be unfair, I gather, because society could not function if everyone disobeyed laws he disapproved of or found disadvantageous. If the government tolerates those few who will not "play the game," it allows them to secure the benefits of everyone else's deference to law, without shouldering the burdens, such as the burden of the draft.

This argument is a serious one. It cannot be answered simply by saying that the dissenters would allow everyone else the privilege of disobeying a law he believed immoral. In fact, few draft dissenters would accept a changed society in which sincere segregationists were free to break civil rights laws they hated. The majority want no such change, in any event, because they think that society would be worse off for it; until they are shown this is wrong, they will expect their officials to punish anyone who assumes a privilege which they, for the general benefit, do not assume.

There is, however, a flaw in the argument. The reasoning contains a hidden assumption that makes it almost entirely irrelevant to the draft cases, and indeed to any serious case of civil disobedience in the United States. The argument assumes that the dissenters know that they are breaking a valid law, and that the privilege they assert is the privilege to do that. Of course, almost everyone who discusses civil disobedience recognizes that in America a law may be invalid because it is unconstitutional. But the critics handle this complexity by arguing on separate hypotheses: If the law is invalid, then no crime is committed, and society may not punish. If the law is valid, then a crime has been committed, and society must punish. This reasoning hides the crucial fact that the validity of the law may be doubtful. The officials and judges may believe that the law is valid, the dissenters may disagree, and both sides may have plausible arguments for their positions. If so, then the issues are different from what they would be if the law were clearly valid or clearly invalid, and the argument of fairness, designed for these alternatives, is irrelevant.

Doubtful law is by no means special or exotic in cases of civil disobedience. On the contrary. In the United States, at least, almost any law which a significant number of people would be tempted to disobey on moral grounds would be doubtful—if not clearly invalid—on constitutional grounds as well. The constitution makes our conventional political morality relevant to the question of validity; any statute that appears to compromise that morality raises constitutional questions, and if the compromise is serious, the constitutional doubts are serious also.

The connection between moral and legal issues is especially clear in the current draft cases. Dissent has largely been based on the following moral objections: (a) The United States is using immoral weapons and tactics in Vietnam. (b) The war has never been endorsed by deliberate, considered, and open vote of the peoples' representatives. (c) The United States has no interest at stake in Vietnam remotely strong enough to justify forcing a segment of its citizens to risk death there. (d) If an army is to be raised to fight that war, it is immoral to raise it by a draft that defers or exempts college students, and thus discriminates against the economically underprivileged. (e) The draft exempts those who object to all wars on religious grounds, but not those who object to particular wars on moral grounds; there is no relevant difference between these positions, and so the draft, by making the distinction, implies that the second group is less worthy of the nation's respect than the first. (f) The law that makes it a crime to counsel draft resistance stifles those who oppose the war, because it is morally impossible to argue that the war is profoundly immoral, without encouraging and assisting those who refuse to fight it.

Lawyers will recognize that these moral positions, if we accept them, provide the basis for the following constitutional arguments: (a) The constitution makes treaties part of the law of the land, and the United States is a party to international conventions and covenants that make illegal the acts of war the dissenters charge the nation with committing. (b) The constitution provides that Congress must declare war; the legal issue of whether our action in Vietnam is a "war" and whether the Tonkin Bay Resolution was a "declaration" is the heart of the moral issue of whether the government has made a deliberate and open decision. (c) Both the due process clause of the Fifth and Fourteenth Amendments and equal protection clause of the Fourteenth Amendment condemn special burdens placed on a selected class of citizens when the burden or the classification is not reasonable; the burden is unreasonable when it patently does not serve the public interest, or when it is vastly disproportionate to the interest served. If our military action in Vietnam is frivolous or perverse, as the dissenters claim, then the burden we place on men of draft age is unreasonable and unconstitutional. (d) In any event, the discrimination in favor of college students denies to the poor the equal protection of the law that is guaranteed by the constitution. (e) If there is no pertinent difference between religious objection to all wars and moral objection to some wars, then the classification the draft makes is arbitrary and unreasonable, and unconstitutional on that ground. The "establishment of religion" clause of the First Amendment forbids governmental pressure in favor of organized religion; if the draft's distinction coerces men in this direction, it is invalid on that count also. (f) The First Amendment also condemns invasions of freedom of speech. If the draft law's prohibition on counseling does inhibit expression of a range of views on the war, it abridges free speech.

The principal counterargument, supporting the view that the courts ought not to hold the draft unconstitutional, also involves moral issues. Under the so-called "political question" doctrine, the courts deny their own jurisdiction to pass on matters—such as foreign or military policy—whose resolution is best assigned to other branches of the government. The Boston court trying the Coffin, Spock case has already declared, on the basis of this doctrine, that it will not hear arguments about the legality of the war. But the Supreme Court has shown itself (in the reapportionment cases, for example) reluctant to refuse jurisdiction when it believed that the gravest issues of political morality were at stake and that no remedy was available through the political process. If the dissenters are right, and the war and the draft are state crimes of profound injustice to a group of citizens, then the argument that the courts must refuse jurisdiction is considerably weakened.

We cannot conclude from these arguments that the draft (or any part of it) is unconstitutional. If the Supreme Court is called upon to rule on the question, it will probably reject some of them, and refuse to consider the others on grounds that they are political. The majority of lawyers would probably agree with this result. But the arguments of unconstitutionality are at least plausible, and a reasonable and competent lawyer might well think that they present a stronger case, on balance, than the counterarguments. If he does, he will consider that the draft is not constitutional, and there will be no way of proving that he is wrong.

Therefore we cannot assume, in judging what to do with the draft dissenters, that they are asserting a privilege to disobey valid laws. We cannot decide that fairness demands their punishment until we try to answer the further question: What should a citizen do when the law is unclear, and when he thinks it allows what others think it does not? I do not mean to ask, of course, what it is *legally* proper for him to do, or what his *legal* rights are—that would be begging the question, because it depends upon whether he is right or they are right. I mean to ask what his proper course is as a citizen, what, in other words, we would consider to be "playing the game." That is a crucial question, because it cannot be unfair not to punish him if he is acting as, given his opinions, we think he should.[1]

There is no obvious answer on which most citizens would readily agree, and that is itself significant. If we examine our

[1] I do not mean to imply that the government should always punish a man who deliberately breaks a law he knows is valid. There may be reasons of fairness or practicality, like those I listed in the third paragraph, for not prosecuting such men. [See my "The Vietnam War and the Right of Resistance," above, for a discussion of this issue. Ed.] But cases like the draft cases present special arguments for tolerance; I want to concentrate on these arguments and therefore have isolated these cases.

legal institutions and practices, however, we shall discover some relevant underlying principles and policies. I shall set out three possible answers to the question, and then try to show which of these best fits our practices and expectations. The three possibilities I want to consider are these:

(1) *If the law is doubtful, and it is therefore unclear whether it permits someone to do what he wants, he should assume the worst, and act on the assumption that it does not. He should obey the executive authorities who command him, even though he thinks they are wrong, while using the political process, if he can, to change the law.*

(2) *If the law is doubtful, he may follow his own judgment, that is, may do what he wants if he believes that the case that the law permits this is stronger than the case that it does not. But he may follow his own judgment only until an authoritative institution, like a court, decides the other way in a case involving him or someone else. Once an institutional decision has been reached, he must abide by that decision, even though he thinks that it was wrong. (There are, in theory, many subdivisions of this second possibility. We may say that the individual's choice is foreclosed by the contrary decision of any court, including the lowest court in the system if the case is not appealed. Or we may require a decision of some particular court or institution. I shall discuss this second possibility in its most liberal form, namely that the individual may properly follow his own judgment until a contrary decision of the highest court competent to pass on the issue, which, in the case of the draft, is the United States Supreme Court.)*

(3) *If the law is doubtful, he may follow his own judgment, even after a contrary decision by the highest competent court. Of course, he must take the contrary decision of any court into account in making his judgment of what the law requires. Otherwise the judgment would not be an honest or reasonable one, because the doctrine of precedent, which is an established part of our legal system, has the effect of allowing the decision of the courts to change the law. Suppose, for example, that a taxpayer believes that he is not required to pay tax on certain forms of income. If the Supreme Court decides to the contrary, he should, taking into account the practice of according great weight to the decisions of the Supreme Court on tax matters, decide that the Court's decision has itself tipped the balance, and that the law now requires him to pay the tax.*

Someone might think that this qualification erases the difference between the third and the second models, but it does not.

The doctrine of precedent gives different weights to the decisions of different courts, and greatest weight to the decisions of the Supreme Court, but it does not make the decision of any court conclusive. Sometimes, even after a contrary Supreme Court decision, an individual may still reasonably believe that the law is on his side; such cases are rare, but they are most likely to occur in disputes over constitutional law when civil disobedience is involved. The Court has shown itself more likely to overrule its past decisions if these have limited important personal or political rights, and it is just these decisions that a dissenter might want to challenge.

We cannot assume, in other words, that the Constitution is always what the Supreme Court says it is. Oliver Wendell Holmes, for example, did not follow such a rule in his famous dissent in the *Gitlow* case. A few years before, in *Abrams,* he had lost his battle to persuade the court that the First Amendment protected an anarchist who had been urging general strikes against the government. A similar issue was presented in *Gitlow,* and Holmes once again dissented. "It is true," he said, "that in my opinion this criterion was departed from [in *Abrams*] but the convictions that I expressed in that case are too deep for it to be possible for me as yet to believe that it . . . settled the law." Holmes voted for acquitting Gitlow, on the ground that what Gitlow had done was no crime, even though the Supreme Court had recently held that it was.

Here then are three possible models for the behavior of dissenters who disagree with the executive authorities when the law is doubtful. Which of them best fits our legal and social practices?

I think it plain that we do not follow the first of these models, that is, that we do not expect citizens to assume the worst. If no court has decided the issue, and a man thinks, on balance, that the law is on his side, most of our lawyers and critics think it perfectly proper for him to follow his own judgment. Even when many disapprove of what he does—such as peddling pornography—they do not think he must desist just because the legality of his conduct is subject to doubt.

It is worth pausing a moment to consider what society would lose if it did follow the first model or, to put the matter the other way, what society gains when people follow their own judgment in cases like this. When the law is uncertain, in the sense that lawyers can reasonably disagree on what a court ought to decide, the reason usually is that different legal principles and policies have collided, and it is unclear how best to accommodate these conflicting principles and policies.

Our practice, in which different parties are encouraged to pursue their own understanding, provides a means of testing relevant hypotheses. If the question is whether a particular rule would have certain undesirable consequences, or whether these consequences would have limited or broad ramifications, then, before the issue is decided, it is useful to know what does in fact take place when some people proceed on that rule. (Much anti-trust and business regulation law has developed through this kind of testing.) If the question is whether and to what degree a particular solution would offend principles of justice or fair play deeply respected by the community, it is useful, again, to experiment by testing the community's response. The extent of community indifference to anti-contraception laws, for example, would never have become established had not some organizations deliberately flouted those laws.

If the first model were followed, we would lose the advantages of these tests. The law would suffer, particularly if this model were applied to constitutional issues. When the validity of a criminal statute is in doubt, the statute will almost always strike some people as being unfair or unjust, because it will infringe some principle of liberty or justice or fairness which they take to be built into the Constitution. If our practice were that whenever a law is doubtful on these grounds, one must act as if it were valid, then the chief vehicle we have for challenging the law on moral grounds would be lost, and over time the law we obeyed would certainly become less fair and just, and the liberty of our citizens would certainly be diminished.

We would lose almost as much if we used a variation of the first model, that a citizen must assume the worst unless he can anticipate that the courts will agree with his view of the law. If everyone deferred to his guess of what the courts would do, society and its law would be poorer. Our assumption in rejecting the first model was that the record a citizen makes in following his own judgment, together with the arguments he makes supporting that judgment when he has the opportunity, are helpful in creating the best judicial decision possible. This remains true even when, at the time the citizen acts, the odds are against his success in court. We must remember, too, that the value of the citizen's example is not exhausted once the decision has been made. Our practices require that the decision be criticized, by the legal profession and the law schools, and the record of dissent may be invaluable here.

Of course a man must consider what the courts will do when he decides whether it would be *prudent* to follow his own judgment. He may have to face jail, bankruptcy, or opprobrium if he does. But it is essential that we separate the calculation of prudence from the question of what, as a good citizen, he may properly do. We are investigating how society ought to treat him when its courts believe that he judged wrong; therefore we must ask what he is justified in doing when his judgment differs from others. We beg the question if we assume that what he may properly do depends on his guess as to how society will treat him.

We must also reject the second model, that if the law is unclear a citizen may properly follow his own judgment until the highest court has ruled that he is wrong. This fails to take into account the fact that any court, including the Supreme Court, may overrule itself. In 1940 the Court decided that a West Virginia law requiring students to salute the Flag was constitutional. In 1943 it reversed itself, and decided that such a statute was unconstitutional after all. What was the duty, as citizens, of those people who in 1941 and 1942 objected to saluting the Flag on grounds of conscience, and thought that the Court's 1940 decision was wrong? We can hardly say that their duty was to follow the first decision. They believed that saluting the Flag was unconscionable, and they believed, reasonably, that no valid law required them to do so. The Supreme Court later decided that in this they were right. The Court did not simply hold that after the second decision failing to salute would not be a crime; it held (as in a case like this it almost always would) that it was no crime after the first decision either.

Some will say that the flag-salute dissenters should have obeyed the Court's first decision, while they worked in the legislatures to have the law repealed, and tried in the courts to find some way to challenge the law again without actually violating it. That would be, perhaps, a plausible recommendation if conscience were not involved, because it would then be arguable that the gain in orderly procedure was worth the personal sacrifice of patience. But conscience was involved, and if the dissenters had obeyed the law while biding their time, they would have suffered the irreparable injury of having done what their conscience forbade them to do. It is one thing to say that an individual must sometimes violate his conscience when he knows that the law commands him to do it. It is quite another to say that he must violate his conscience even when he reasonably believes that the law does not require it, because it would inconvenience his fellow citizens if he took the most direct, and perhaps the only, method of attempting to show that he is right and they are wrong.

Since a court may overrule itself, the same reasons we listed for rejecting the first model count against the second as well. If we did not have the pressure of dissent, we would not have a dramatic statement of the degree to which a court decision against the dissenter is felt to be wrong, a demonstration that is surely pertinent to the question of whether it was right. We would increase the chance of being governed by rules that offend the principles we claim to serve.

These considerations force us, I think, from the second model, but some will want to substitute a variation of it. They will argue that once the Supreme Court has decided that a criminal law is valid, then citizens have a duty to abide by that decision until they have a reasonable belief, not merely that the decision is a bad law, but that the Supreme Court is likely to overrule it. Under this view the West Virginia dissenters who refused to salute the Flag in 1942 were acting properly, because they might reasonably have anticipated that the Court would change its mind. But if the Court were to hold the draft laws constitutional, it would be improper to continue to challenge these laws, because there would be no great likelihood that the Court would soon change its mind. This suggestion must also be rejected, however. For once we say that a citizen may properly follow his own judgment of the law, in spite of his judgment that the courts will probably find against him, there is no plausible reason why he should act differently because a contrary decision is already on the books.

Thus the third model, or something close to it, seems to be the fairest statement of a man's social duty in our community. A citizen's allegiance is to the law, not to any particular person's view of what the law is, and he does not behave unfairly so long as he proceeds on his own considered and reasonable view of what the law requires. Let me repeat (because it is crucial) that this is not the same as saying that an individual may disregard what the courts have said. The doctrine of precedent lies near the core of our legal system, and no one can make a reasonable effort to follow the law unless he grants the courts the general power to alter it by their decisions. But if the issue is one touching fundamental personal or political rights, and it is arguable that the Supreme Court has made a mistake, a man is within his social rights in refusing to accept that decision as conclusive.

One large question remains before we can apply these observations to the problems of draft resistance. I have been talking about the case of a man who believes that the law is not what other people think, or what the courts have held. This description may fit some of those who disobey the draft laws out of conscience, but it does not fit most of them. Most of the dissenters are not lawyers or political philosophers; they believe that the laws on the books are immoral, and inconsistent with their country's legal ideals, but they have not considered the question of whether they may be invalid as well. Of what relevance to their situation, then, is the proposition that one may properly follow one's own view of the law?

To answer this, I shall have to return to the point I made earlier. The Constitution, through the due process clause, the equal protection clause, the First Amendment, and the other provisions I mentioned, injects an extraordinary amount of our political morality into the issue of whether a law is valid. The statement that most draft dissenters are unaware that the law is invalid therefore needs qualification. They hold beliefs that, if true, strongly support the view that law is on their side; the fact that they have not reached that further conclusion can be traced, in at least most cases, to their lack of legal sophistication. If we believe that when the law is doubtful people who follow their own judgment of the law may be acting properly, it would seem wrong not to extend that view to those dissenters whose judgments come to the same thing. No part of the case that I made for the third model would entitle us to distinguish them from their more knowledgeable colleagues.

We can draw several tentative conclusions from the argument so far: When the law is uncertain, in the sense that a plausible case can be made on both sides, then a citizen who follows his own judgment is not behaving unfairly. Our practices permit and encourage him to follow his own judgment in such cases. For that reason, our government has a special responsibility to try to protect him, and soften his predicament, whenever it can do so without great damage to other policies. It does not follow that the government can guarantee him immunity—it cannot adopt the rule that it will prosecute no one who acts out of conscience, or convict no one who reasonably disagrees with the courts. That would paralyze the government's ability to carry out its policies; it would, moreover, throw away the most important benefit of following the third model. If the state never prosecuted, then the courts could not act on the experience and the arguments the dissent has generated. But it does follow that when the practical reasons for prosecuting are relatively weak in a particular case, or can be met in other ways, the path of fairness lies in tolerance. The popular view that the law is the law and must always be enforced refuses to distinguish the man who acts on his own judgment of a doubtful law, and thus behaves as our practices provide, from the common criminal. I know of no reason, short of moral blindness, for not drawing a distinction in principle between the two cases.

I anticipate a philosophical objection to these conclusions: that I am treating law as a "brooding omnipresence in the sky." I have spoken of people making judgments about what the law requires, even in cases in which the law is unclear and undemonstrable. I have spoken of cases in which a man might think that the law requires one thing, even though the Supreme Court has said that it requires another, and even when it was not likely that the Supreme Court would soon change its mind. I will therefore be charged with the view that there is always a "right answer" to a legal problem to be found in natural law or locked up in some transcendental strongbox.

The strongbox theory of law is, of course, nonsense. When I say that people hold views on the law when the law is doubtful, and that these views are not merely predictions of what the courts will hold, I intend no such metaphysics. I mean only to summarize as accurately as I can many of the practices that are part of our legal process.

Lawyers and judges make statements of legal right and duty, even when they know these are not demonstrable, and support them with arguments even when they know that these arguments will not appeal to everyone. They make these arguments to one another, in the professional journals, in the classroom, and in the courts. They respond to these arguments, when others make them, by judging them good or bad or mediocre. In so doing they assume that some arguments for a given doubtful position are better than others. They also assume that the case on one side of a doubtful proposition may be stronger than the case on the other, which is what I take a claim of law in a doubtful case to mean. They distinguish, without too much difficulty, these arguments from predictions of what the courts will decide.

These practices are poorly represented by the theory that judgments of law on doubtful issues are nonsense, or are merely predictions of what the courts will do. Those who hold such theories cannot deny the fact of these practices; perhaps these theorists mean that the practices are not sensible, because they are based on suppositions that do not hold, or for some other reason. But this makes their objection mysterious, because they never specify what they take the purposes underlying these practices to be; and unless these goals are specified, one cannot decide whether the practices are sensible. I understand these underlying purposes to be those I described earlier: the development and testing of the law through experimentation by citizens and through the adversary process.

Our legal system pursues these goals by inviting citizens to decide the strengths and weaknesses of legal arguments for themselves, or through their own counsel, and to act on these judgments, although that permission is qualified by the limited threat that they may suffer if the courts do not agree. Success in this strategy depends on whether there is sufficient agreement within the community on what counts as a good or bad argument, so that, although different people will reach different judgments, these differences will be neither so profound nor so frequent as to make the system unworkable, or dangerous for those who act by their own lights. I believe there is sufficient agreement on the criteria of the argument to avoid these traps, although one of the main tasks of legal philosophy is to exhibit and clarify these criteria. In any event, the practices I have described have not yet been shown to be misguided; they therefore must count in determining whether it is just and fair to be lenient to those who break what others think is the law.

I have said that the government has a special responsibility to those who act on a reasonable judgment that a law is invalid. It should make accommodation for them as far as possible, when this is consistent with other policies. It may be difficult to decide what the government ought to do, in the name of that responsibility, in particular cases. The decision will be a matter of balance, and flat rules will not help. Still, some principles can be set out.

I shall start with the prosecutor's decision whether to press charges. He must balance both his responsibility to be lenient and the risk that convictions will rend the society, against the damage to the law's policy that may follow if he leaves the dissenters alone. In making his calculation he must consider not only the extent to which others will be harmed, but also how the law evaluates that harm; and he must therefore make the following distinction. Every rule of law is supported, and presumably justified, by a set of policies it is supposed to advance and principles it is supposed to respect. Some rules (the laws prohibiting murder and theft, for example) are supported by the proposition that the individuals protected have a moral right to be free from the harm proscribed. Other rules (the more technical antitrust rules, for example) are not supported by any supposition of an underlying right; their support comes chiefly from the alleged utility of the economic and social policies they promote. These may be supplemented with moral principles (like the view that it is a harsh business practice to undercut a weak competitor's prices) but these fall short of recognizing a moral right against the harm in question.

The point of the distinction here is this: if a particular rule of law represents an official decision that individuals have a moral right to be free from some harm, then that is a powerful argument against tolerating violations that inflict those injuries. Laws protecting people from personal injury or the destruction of their property, for example, do represent that sort of decision, and this is a very strong argument against tolerating civil disobedience that involves violence.

It may be controversial, of course, whether a law does rest on the assumption of a moral right. The question is whether it is reasonable to suppose, from the background and administration of the law, that its authors recognized such a right. These are cases, in addition to rules against violence, where it is plain that they did; the civil rights laws are examples. Many sincere and ardent segregationists believe that the civil rights laws and decisions are unconstitutional, because they compromise principles of local government and of freedom of association. This is an arguable, though not a persuasive, view. But these laws and decisions clearly embody the view that Negroes, as individuals, have a right not to be segregated. They do not rest simply on the judgment that other national policies are best pursued by preventing racial segregation. If we take no action against the man who blocks the school house door, therefore, we violate the moral rights, confirmed by law, of the schoolgirl he blocks. The responsibility of leniency cannot go this far.

The schoolgirl's position is different, however, from that of the draftee, who may be called up sooner or given a more dangerous post if draft offenders are not punished. The draft laws, taken as a whole and with an eye to their administration, cannot be said to reflect the judgment that a man has a moral right to be drafted only after certain other men or groups have been called. The draft classifications, and the order-of-call within classifications, are arranged for social and administrative convenience. They also reflect considerations of fairness, like the proposition that a mother who has lost one of two sons in war ought not to be made to risk losing the other. But they presuppose no fixed rights. The draft boards are given considerable discretion in the classification process, and the army, of course, has almost complete discretion in assigning dangerous posts. If the prosecutor tolerates draft offenders, he makes small shifts in the law's calculations of fairness and utility.

These may cause disadvantage to others in the pool of draftees but that is a different matter from contradicting their moral rights.

This difference between segregation and the draft is not an accident of how the laws happen to have been written. It would run counter to a century of practice to suppose that citizens have moral rights with respect to the order in which they are called to serve; the lottery system of selection, for example, would be abhorrent under that supposition. If our history had been different, and if the community had recognized such a moral right, it seems fair to suppose that some of the draft dissenters, at least, would have modified their acts so as to try to respect these rights. So it is wrong to analyze draft cases in the same way as cases of violence or civil rights cases, as many critics do when considering whether tolerance is justified. I do not mean that fairness to others is irrelevant in draft cases; it must be taken into account, and balanced against fairness to dissenters and the long-term benefit to society. But it does not play the commanding role here that it does when rights are at stake.

Where, then, does the balance of fairness and utility lie in the case of those who counsel draft resistance? If these men had encouraged violence or otherwise trespassed on the rights of others, then there would be a strong case for prosecution. But in the absence of such actions, the balance of fairness and utility seems to me to lie the other way, and I therefore think that the decision to prosecute Coffin, Spock, Raskin, Goodman, and Ferber was wrong. It may be argued that if those who counsel draft resistance are free from prosecution, the number who resist induction will increase; but it will not, I think, increase much beyond the number of those who would resist in any event.

If I am wrong, and there is much greater resistance, then a sense of this residual discontent is of importance to policy makers, and it ought not to be hidden under a ban on speech. Conscience is deeply involved—it is hard to believe that many who counsel resistance do so on any other grounds. The case is strong that the laws making counseling a crime are unconstitutional; even those who do not find the case persuasive will admit that its arguments have substance. The harm to potential draftees, both those who may be persuaded to resist and those who may be called earlier because others have been persuaded, is remote and speculative.

The cases of men who refuse induction when drafted are more complicated. The crucial question is whether a failure to prosecute will lead to wholesale refusals to serve. It may not—there are social pressures, including the threat of career disadvantages, that would force many young Americans to serve if drafted, even if they knew they would not go to jail if they refused. If the number would not much increase, then the state should leave the dissenters alone, and I see no great harm in delaying any prosecution until the effect of that policy becomes clearer. If the number of those who refuse induction turns out to be large, this would argue for prosecution. But it would also make the problem academic, because if there were sufficient dissent to bring us to that pass, it would be most difficult to pursue the war in any event, except under a near-totalitarian regime.

There may seem to be a paradox in these conclusions. I argued earlier that when the law is unclear citizens have the right to follow their own judgment, partly on the grounds that this practice helps to shape issues for adjudication; now I propose a course that eliminates or postpones adjudication. But the contradiction is only apparent. It does not follow from the fact that our practice facilitates adjudication, and renders it more useful in developing the law, that a trial should follow whenever citizens do act by their own lights. The question arises in each case whether the issues are ripe for adjudication, and whether adjudication would settle these issues in a manner that would decrease the chance of, or remove the grounds for, further dissent.

In the draft cases, the answer to both these questions is negative: There is much ambivalence about the war just now, and uncertainty and ignorance about the scope of the moral issues involved in the draft. It is far from the best time for a court to pass on these issues, and tolerating dissent for a time is one way of allowing the debate to continue until it has produced something clearer. Moreover, it is plain that an adjudication of the constitutional issues now will not settle the law. Those who have doubts whether the draft is constitutional will have the same doubts even if the Supreme Court says that it is. This is one of these cases, touching fundamental rights, in which our practices of precedent will encourage these doubts. Certainly this will be so if, as seems likely, the Supreme Court appeals to the political question doctrine, and refuses to pass on the more serious constitutional issues.

Even if the prosecutor does not act, however, the underlying problem will be only temporarily relieved. So long as the law appears to make acts of dissent criminal, a man of conscience will face danger. What can Congress, which shares the responsibility of leniency, do to lessen this danger?

Congress can review the laws in question to see how much accommodation can be given the dissenters. Every program a legislature adopts is a mixture of policies and restraining principles. We accept loss of efficiency in crime detection and urban renewal, for example, so that we can respect the rights of accused criminals and compensate property owners for their damages. Congress may properly defer to its responsibility toward the dissenters by adjusting or compromising other policies. The relevant questions are these: What means can be found for allowing the greatest possible tolerance of conscientious dissent while minimizing its impact on policy? How strong is the government's responsibility for leniency in this case—how deeply is conscience involved, and how strong is the case that the law is invalid after all? How important is the policy in question—is interference with that policy too great a price to pay? These questions are no doubt too simple, but they suggest the heart of the choices that must be made.

For the same reasons that those who counsel resistance should not be prosecuted, I think that the law that makes this a crime should be repealed. The case is strong that this law abridges free speech. It certainly coerces conscience, and it probably serves no beneficial effect. If counseling would persuade only a few to resist who otherwise would not, the value of the restraint is small; if counseling would persuade many, that is an important political fact that should be known.

The issues are more complex, again, in the case of draft resistance itself. Those who believe that the war in Vietnam is itself a grotesque blunder will favor any change in the law that makes peace more likely. But if we take the position of those who think the war is necessary, then we must admit that a policy that continues the draft but wholly exempts dissenters would be unwise. Two less drastic alternatives might be considered, however: a volunteer army, and an expanded conscientious objecter category that includes those who find this war immoral. There is much to be said against both proposals, but once the requirement of respect for dissent is recognized, the balance of principle may be tipped in their favor.

So the case for not prosecuting conscientious draft offenders, and for changing the laws in their favor, is a strong one. It would be unrealistic to expect this policy to prevail, however, for political pressures now oppose it. Relatively few of those who have refused induction have been indicted so far, but the pace of prosecution is quickening, and many more indictments are expected if the resistance many college seniors have pledged does in fact develop. The Coffin, Spock trial continues, although when the present steps toward peace negotiation were announced, many lawyers had hoped it would be dropped or delayed. There is no sign of any movement to amend the draft laws in the way I have suggested.

We must consider, therefore, what the courts can and should now do. A court might, of course, uphold the arguments that the draft laws are in some way unconstitutional, in general or as applied to the defendants in the case at hand. Or it may acquit the defendants because the facts necessary for conviction are not proved. I shall not argue the constitutional issues, or the facts of any particular case. I want instead to suggest that a court ought not to convict, at least in some circumstances, even if it sustains the statutes and finds the facts as charged. The Supreme Court has not ruled on the chief arguments that the present draft is unconstitutional, nor has it held that these arguments raise poltical questions that are not relevant to its jurisdiction. If the alleged violations take place before the Supreme Court has decided these issues, and the case reaches that Court, there are strong reasons why the Court should acquit even if it does then sustain the draft. It ought to acquit on the ground that before its decision the validity of the draft was doubtful, and it is unfair to punish men for disobeying a doubtful law.

There would be precedent for a decision along these lines. The Court has several times reversed criminal convictions, on due process grounds, because the law in question was too vague. (It has overturned convictions, for example, under laws that made it a crime to charge "unreasonable prices" or to be a member of a "gang.") Conviction under a vague criminal law offends the moral and political ideals of due process in two ways. First, it places a citizen in the unfair position of either actir.g at his peril or accepting a more stringent restriction on his life than the legislature may have authorized: As I argued earlier, it is not acceptable, as a model of social behavior, that in such cases he ought to assume the worst. Second, it gives power to the prosecutor and the courts to make criminal law, by opting for one or the other possible interpretations after the event. This would be a delegation of authority by the legislature that is inconsistent with our scheme of separation of powers.

Conviction under a criminal law whose terms are not vague, but whose constitutional validity is doubtful, offends due process in the first of these ways. It forces a citizen to assume the worst, or act at his peril. It offends due process in something like the second way as well. Most citizens would be deterred by a doubtful statute if they were to risk jail by violating it. Congress, and not the courts, would then be the effective voice in deciding the constitutionality of criminal enactments, and this also violates the separation of powers.

If acts of dissent continue to occur after the Supreme Court has ruled that the laws are valid, or that the political question doctrine applies, then acquittal on the grounds I have described is no longer appropriate. The Court's decision will not have finally settled the law, for the reasons given earlier, but the Court will have done all that can be done to settle it. The courts may still exercise their sentencing discretion, however, and impose minimal or suspended sentences as a mark of respect for the dissenters' position.

Some lawyers will be shocked by my general conclusion that we have a responsibility toward those who disobey the draft laws out of conscience, and that we may be required not to prosecute them, but rather to change our laws or adjust our sentencing procedures to accommodate them. The simple Draconian propositions, that crime must be punished, and that he who misjudges the law must take the consequences, have an extraordinary hold on the professional as well as the popular imagination. But the rule of law is more complex and more intelligent than that and it is important that it survive.

Postscript [1970]

The Nixon Administration, according to *The New York Times,* has sharply increased the number of prosecutions for draft offenses. The current rate of prosecution is well above the rate of prosecution when this article was written. The administration has not increased prosecutions in response to practical dangers of the sort I said might justify prosecution, for the draft call reductions and troop withdrawals it has announced would, if anything, reduce these dangers. On the contrary, it seems to have acted in the name of that maxim which I argued is too simple for an intelligent and fair legal policy, the maxim that the law is the law and must always be enforced.

Peter Kropotkin

Law and Authority

I

"When ignorance reigns in society and disorder in the minds **131** of men, laws are multiplied, legislation is expected to do everything, and each fresh law being a fresh miscalculation, men are continually led to demand from it what can proceed only from themselves, from their own education and their own morality." It is no revolutionist who says this, not even a reformer. It is the jurist, Dalloy, author of the collection of French law known as *Répertoire de la Législation.* And yet, though these lines were written by a man who was himself a maker and admirer of law, they perfectly represent the abnormal condition of our society.

In existing States a fresh law is looked upon as a remedy for evil. Instead of themselves altering what is bad, people begin by demanding a *law* to alter it. If the road between two villages is impassable, the peasant says:—"There should be a law about parish roads." If a park-keeper takes advantage of the want of spirit in those who follow him with servile observance and insults one of them, the insulted man says, "There should be a law to enjoin more politeness upon park-keepers." If there is stagnation in agriculture or commerce, the husbandman, cattle-breeder, or corn speculator argues, "It is protective legislation that we require." Down to the old clothesman there is not one who does not demand a law to

"Law and Authority," written in English, was first published as a pamphlet from Freedom Press, London, in 1886. It has recently been reprinted in the collection, *Kropotkin's Revolutionary Pamphlets,* edited by Roger Baldwin, from Benjamin Blom, Inc., New York, 1968. It is reprinted here (abridged) by permission of Benjamin Blom, Inc. Peter Kropotkin (1842–1921) was born in Moscow, a Prince of the Russian nobility, and during his childhood was a page of the Emperor. During his thirties, he became a revolutionary anarchist. He was jailed in St. Petersburg, escaped after two years, and made his way to England. Though a distinguished geographer, his first concern was politics. He wrote extensive philosophical defenses of anarchism and was also involved in political organization and activity. He lived and visited in a variety of countries (including America). He returned to Russia after the Revolution, but was gravely disturbed that the Soviet Government was developing that very kind of "law and authority" which he had always opposed.

protect his own little trade. If the employer lowers wages or increases the hours of labor, the politician in embryo exclaims, "We must have a law to put all that to rights." In short, a law everywhere and for everything! A law about fashions, a law about mad dogs, a law about virtue, a law to put a stop to all the vices and all the evils which result from human indolence and cowardice.

We are so perverted by an education which from infancy seeks to kill in us the spirit of revolt, and to develop that of submission to authority; we are so perverted by this existence under the ferrule of a law, which regulates every event in life —our birth, our education, our development, our love, our friendship—that, if this state of things continues, we shall lose all initiative, all habit of thinking for ourselves. Our society seems no longer able to understand that it is possible to exist otherwise than under the reign of law, elaborated by a representative government and administered by a handful of rulers. And even when it has gone so far as to emancipate itself from the thralldom, its first care has been to reconstitute it immediately. "The Year I of Liberty" has never lasted more than a day, for after proclaiming it men put themselves the very next morning under the yoke of law and authority.

Indeed, for some thousands of years, those who govern us have done nothing but ring the changes upon "Respect for law, obedience to authority." This is the moral atmosphere in which parents bring up their children, and school only serves to confirm the impression. Cleverly assorted scraps of spurious science are inculcated upon the children to prove necessity of law; obedience to the law is made a religion; moral goodness and the law of the masters are fused into one and the same divinity. The historical hero of the schoolroom is the man who obeys the law, and defends it against rebels.

Later when we enter upon public life, society and literature, impressing us day by day and hour by hour as the water-drop hollows the stone, continue to inculcate the same prejudice. Books of history, of political science, of social economy, are stuffed with this respect for law. Even the physical sciences have been pressed into the service by introducing artificial modes of expression, borrowed from theology and arbitrary power, into knowledge which is purely the result of observation. Thus our intelligence is successfully befogged, and always to maintain our respect for law. The same work is done by newspapers. They have not an article which does not preach respect for law, even where the third page proves every day the imbecility of that law, and shows how it is dragged through every variety of mud and filth by those charged with its administration. Servility before the law has become a virtue, and I doubt if there was ever even a revolutionist who did not begin in his youth as the defender of law against what are generally called "abuses," although these last are inevitable consequences of the law itself. . . .

To understand this [worship of law], we must transport ourselves in imagination into the eighteenth century. Our hearts must have ached at the story of the atrocities committed by the all-powerful nobles of that time upon the men and women of the people before we can understand what must have been the magic influence upon the peasant's mind of the words, "Equality before the law, obedience to the law without distinction of birth or fortune." He who until then had been treated more cruelly than a beast, he who had never had any rights, he who had never obtained justice against the most revolting actions on the part of a noble, unless in revenge he killed him and was hanged—he saw himself recognized by this maxim, at least in theory, at least with regard to his personal rights, as the equal of his lord. Whatever this law might be, it promised to affect lord and peasant alike; it proclaimed the equality of rich and poor before the judge. The promise was a lie, and to-day we know it; but at that period it was an advance, a homage to justice, as hypocrisy is a homage rendered to truth. This is the reason that when the saviors of the menaced middle class (the Robespierres and the Dantons) took their stand upon the writings of the Rousseaus and the Voltaires, and proclaimed "respect for law, the same for every man," the people accepted the compromise; for their revolutionary impetus had already spent its force in the contest with a foe whose ranks drew closer day by day; they bowed their neck beneath the yoke of law to save themselves from the arbitrary power of their lords.

The middle class has ever since continued to make the most of this maxim, which with another principle, that of representative government, sums up the whole philosophy of the bourgeois age, the nineteenth century. It has preached this doctrine in its schools, it has propagated it in its writings, it has moulded its art and science to the same purpose, it has thrust its beliefs into every hole and corner—like a pious Englishwoman, who slips tracts under the door—and it has done all this so successfully that today we behold the issue in the detestable fact that men who long for freedom begin the attempt to obtain it by entreating their masters to be kind enough to protect them by modifying the laws which these masters themselves have created!

But times and tempers are changed. Rebels are everywhere to be found who no longer wish to obey the law without knowing whence it comes, what are its uses, and whither arises the obligation to submit to it, and the reverence with which it is encompassed. The rebels of our day are criticizing the very foundations of society which have hitherto been held sacred, and first and foremost amongst them that fetish, law.

The critics analyze the sources of law, and find there either a god, product of the terrors of the savage, and stupid, paltry and malicious as the priests who vouch for its supernatural origin, or else, bloodshed, conquest by fire and sword. They study the characteristics of law, and instead of perpetual growth corresponding to that of the human race, they find its distinctive traits to be immobility, a tendency to crystallize what should be modified and developed day by day. They ask how law has been maintained, and in its service they see the atrocities of Byzantinism, the cruelties of the Inquisition, the tortures of the middle ages, living flesh torn by the lash of the executioner, chains, clubs, axes, the gloomy dungeons of prisons, agony, curses and tears. In our own days they see, as before, the axe, the cord, the rifle, the prison; on the one hand, the brutalized prisoner, reduced to the condition of a caged beast by the debasement of his whole moral being, and on the other, the judge, stripped of every feeling which does honor to human nature, living like a visionary in a world of legal fictions, revelling in the infliction of imprisonment and death, without even suspecting, in the cold malignity of his madness, the abyss of degradation into which he has himself fallen before the eyes of those whom he condemns.

They see a race of law-makers legislating without knowing what their laws are about; today voting a law on the sanitation of towns, without the faintest notion of hygiene, tomorrow making regulations for the armament of troops, without so much as understanding a gun; making laws about teaching and education without ever having given a lesson of any sort, or even an honest education to their own children; legislating at random in all directions, but never forgetting the penalties to be meted out to ragamuffins, the prison and the galleys, which are to be the portion of men a thousand times less immoral than these legislators themselves.

Finally, they see the jailer on the way to lose all human feeling, the detective trained as a blood-hound, the police spy despising himself; "informing," metamorphosed into a virtue; corruption, erected into a system; all the vices, all the evil qualities of mankind countenanced and cultivated to insure the triumph of law.

All this we see, and, therefore, instead of inanely repeating the old formula, "Respect the law," we say, "Despise law and all its attributes!" In place of the cowardly phrase, "Obey the law," our cry is "Revolt against all laws!"

Only compare the misdeeds accomplished in the name of each law with the good it has been able to effect, and weigh carefully both good and evil, and you will see if we are right.

II

Relatively speaking, law is a product of modern times. For ages and ages mankind lived without any written law, even that graved in symbols upon the entrance stones of a temple. During that period, human relations were simply regulated by customs, habits and usages, made sacred by constant repetition, and acquired by each person in childhood, exactly as he learned how to obtain his food by hunting, cattle-rearing or agriculture.

All human societies have passed through this primitive phase, and to this day a large proportion of mankind have no written law. Every tribe has its own manners and customs; customary law, as the jurists say. It has social habits, and that suffices to maintain cordial relations between the inhabitants of the village, the members of the tribe or community. . . .

Two distinctly marked currents of custom are revealed by analysis of the usages of primitive people.

As man does not live in a solitary state, habits and feelings develop within him which are useful for the preservation of society and the propagation of the race. Without social feelings and usages, life in common would have been absolutely impossible. It is not law which has established them; they are anterior to all law. Neither is it religion which has ordained them; they are anterior to all religions. They are found amongst all animals living in society. They are spontaneously developed by the very nature of things, like those habits in animals which men call instinct. They spring from a process of evolution, which is useful, and, indeed, necessary, to keep society together in the struggle it is forced to maintain for existence. Savages end by no longer eating one another because they find it in the long run more advantageous to devote themselves to some sort of cultivation than to enjoy the pleasure of feasting upon the flesh of an aged relative once a year. Many travelers have depicted the manners of absolutely independent tribes, where laws and chiefs are unknown, but where the members of the tribe have given up stabbing one another in every dispute, because the habit of living in society has ended by developing certain feelings of fraternity and oneness of interest, and they prefer appealing to a third person to settle their differences. The hospitality of primitive peoples, respect for human life, the sense of reciprocal obligation, compassion for the weak, courage, extending even to the sacrifice of self for others which is first learnt for the sake of children and friends, and later for that of members of the same community—all these qualities are developed in man anterior to all law, independently of all religion, as in the case of the social animals. Such feelings and practices are the inevitable results of social life. Without being, as say priests and metaphysicians, inherent in man, such qualities are the consequence of life in common.

But side by side with these customs, necessary to the life of societies and the preservation of the race, other desires, other passions, and therefore other habits and customs, are evolved in human association. The desire to dominate others and impose one's own will upon them; the desire to seize upon the products of the labor of a neighboring tribe; the desire to surround oneself with comforts without producing anything, while slaves provide their master with the means of procuring every sort of pleasure and luxury—these selfish, personal desires give rise to another current of habits and customs. The priest and the warrior, the charlatan who makes a profit out of superstition, and after freeing himself from the fear of the devil cultivates it in others; and the bully, who procures the invasion and pillage of his neighbors that he may return laden with booty and followed by slaves. These two, hand in hand, have succeeded in imposing upon primitive society customs advantageous to both of them, but tending to perpetuate their domination of the masses. Profiting by the indolence, the fears, the inertia of the crowd, and thanks to the continual repetition of the same acts, they have permanently established customs which have become a solid basis for their own domination.

For this purpose, they would have made use, in the first place, of that tendency to run in a groove, so highly developed in mankind. In children and all savages it attains striking proportions, and it may also be observed in animals. Man, when he is at all superstitious, is always afraid to introduce any sort of change into existing conditions; he generally venerates what is ancient. "Our fathers did so and so; they got on pretty well; they brought you up; they were not unhappy; do the same!" the old say to the young every time the latter wish to alter things. The unknown frightens them, they prefer to cling to the past even when that past represents poverty, oppression and slavery.

It may even be said that the more miserable a man is, the more he dreads every sort of change, lest it may make him more wretched still. Some ray of hope, a few scraps of comfort, must penetrate his gloomy abode before he can begin to desire better things, to criticize the old ways of living, and prepare to imperil them for the sake of bringing about a change. So long as he is not imbued with hope, so long as he is not freed from the tutelage of those who utilize his superstition and his fears, he prefers remaining in his former position. If the young desire any change, the old raise a cry of alarm against the innovators. Some savages would rather die than transgress the customs of their country because they have been told from childhood that the least infraction of established routine would bring ill-luck and ruin the whole tribe. Even in the present day, what numbers of politicians, economists, and would-be revolutionists act under the same impression, and cling to a vanishing past. How many care only to seek for precedents. How many fiery innovators are mere copyists of bygone revolutions.

The spirit of routine, originating in superstition, indolence, and cowardice, has in all times been the mainstay of oppression. In primitive human societies it was cleverly turned to account by priests and military chiefs. They perpetuated customs useful only to themselves, and succeeded in imposing them on the whole tribe. So long as this conservative spirit could be exploited so as to assure the chief in his encroachments upon individual liberty, so long as the only inequalities between men were the work of nature, and these were not increased a hundred-fold by the concentration of power and wealth, there was no need for law and the formidable paraphernalia of tribunals and ever-augmenting penalties to enforce it.

But as society became more and more divided into two hostile classes, one seeking to establish its domination, the other struggling to escape, the strife began. Now the conqueror was in a hurry to secure the results of his actions in a permanent form, he tried to place them beyond question, to make them holy and venerable by every means in his power. Law made its appearance under the sanction of the priest, and the warrior's club was placed at its service. Its office was to render immutable such customs as were to the advantage of the dominant minority. Military authority undertook to ensure obedience. This new function was a fresh guarantee to the power of the warrior; now he had not only mere brute force at his service; he was the defender of law.

If law, however, presented nothing but a collection of prescriptions serviceable to rulers, it would find some difficulty in insuring acceptance and obedience. Well, the legislators confounded in one code the two currents of custom of which we have just been speaking, the maxims which represent principles of morality and social union wrought out as a result of life in common, and the mandates which are meant to ensure external existence to inequality. Customs, absolutely essential to the very being of society, are, in the code, cleverly intermingled with usages imposed by the ruling caste, and both claim equal respect from the crowd. "Do not kill," says the code, and hastens to add, "And pay tithes to the priest." "Do not steal," says the code, and immediately after, "He who refuses to pay taxes, shall have his hand struck off."

Such was law; and it has maintained its two-fold character to this day. Its origin is the desire of the ruling class to give permanence to customs imposed by themselves for their own advantage. Its character is the skillful commingling of customs useful to society, customs which have no need of law to insure respect, with other customs useful only to rulers, injurious to the mass of the people, and maintained only by the fear of punishment.

Like individual capital, which was born of fraud and violence, and developed under the auspices of authority, law has no title to the respect of men. Born of violence and superstition, and established in the interests of consumer, priest and rich exploiter, it must be utterly destroyed on the day when the people desire to break their chains. . . .

III

. . . The great [French] Revolution began the demolition of this framework of law, bequeathed to us by feudalism and royalty. But after having demolished some portions of the ancient edifice, the Revolution delivered over the power of law-making to the bourgeoisie, who, in their turn, began to raise a fresh framework of laws intended to maintain and perpetuate middle-class domination among the masses. Their parliament makes laws right and left, and mountains of law accumulate with frightful rapidity. But what *are* all these laws at bottom?

The major portion have but one object—to protect private property, i. e., wealth acquired by the exploitations of man by man. Their aim is to open out to capital fresh fields for exploitation, and to sanction the new forms which that exploitation continually assumes, as capital swallows up another branch of human activity, railways, telegraphs, electric light, chemical industries, the expression of man's thought in literature and science, etc. The object of the rest of these laws is fundamentally the same. They exist to keep up the machinery of government which serves to secure to capital the exploitation and monopoly of the wealth produced. Magistrature, police, army, public instruction, finance, all serve one God—capital; all have but one object—to facilitate the exploitation of the worker by the capitalist. Analyze all the laws passed and you will find nothing but this.

The protection of the person, which is put forward as the true mission of law, occupies an imperceptible space among them, for, in existing society, assaults upon the person directly dictated by hatred and brutality tend to disappear. Nowadays, if anyone is murdered, it is generally for the sake of robbing him; rarely because of personal vengeance. But if this class of crimes and misdemeanors is continually diminishing, we certainly do not owe the change to legislation. It is due to the growth of humanitarianism in our societies, to our increasingly social habits rather than to the prescriptions of our laws. Repeal tomorrow every law dealing with the protection of the person, and tomorrow stop all proceedings for assault, and the number of attempts dictated by personal vengeance and by brutality would not be augmented by one single instance.

It will perhaps be objected that during the last fifty years, a good many liberal laws have been enacted. But, if these laws are analyzed, it will be discovered that this liberal legislation consists in the repeal of the laws bequeathed to us by the barbarism of preceding centuries. Every liberal law, every radical program, may be summed up in these words,—abolition of laws grown irksome to the middle-class itself, and return and extension to all citizens of liberties enjoyed by the townships of the twelfth century. The abolition of capital punishment, trial by jury for all "crimes" (there was a more liberal jury in the twelfth century), the election of magistrates, the right of bringing public officials to trial, the abolition of standing armies, free instruction, etc., everything that is pointed out as an invention of modern liberalism, is but a return to the freedom which existed before church and king had laid hands upon every manifestation of human life.

Thus the protection of exploitation directly by laws on property, and indirectly by the maintenance of the State is both the spirit and the substance of our modern codes, and the one function of our costly legislative machinery. But it is time we gave up being satisfied with mere phrases, and learned to appreciate their real significance. The law, which on its first appearance presented itself as a compendium of customs useful for the preservation of society, is now perceived to be nothing but an instrument for the maintenance of exploitation and the domination of the toiling masses by rich idlers. At the present day its civilizing mission is *nil;* it has but one object,—to bolster up exploitation.

This is what is told us by history as to the development of law. Is it in virtue of this history that we are called upon to respect it? Certainly not. It has no more title to respect than capital, the fruit of pillage. And the first duty of the revolution will be to make a bonfire of all existing laws as it will of all titles to property.

IV

The millions of laws which exist for the regulation of humanity appear upon investigation to be divided into three principal categories: protection of property, protection of persons, protection of government. And by analyzing each of these three categories, we arrive at the same logical and necessary conclusion: *the uselessness and hurtfulness of law.*

Socialists know what is meant by protection of property. Laws on property are not made to guarantee either to the individual or to society the enjoyment of the produce of their own labor. On the contrary, they are made to rob the producer of a part of what he has created, and to secure to certain other people that portion of the produce which they have stolen either from the producer or from society as a whole. When, for example, the law establishes Mr. So-and-So's right to a house, it is not establishing his right to a cottage he has built for himself, or to a house he has erected with the help of some of his friends. In that case no one would have disputed his right. On the contrary, the law is establishing his right to a house which is *not* the product of his labor; first of all because he has had it built for him by others to whom he has not paid the full value of their work, and next because that house represents a social value which he could not have produced for himself. The law is establishing his right to what belongs to everybody in general and to nobody in particular. The same house built in the midst of Siberia would not have the value it possesses in a large town, and, as we know, that value arises from the labor of something like fifty generations of men who have built the town, beautified it, supplied it with water and gas, fine promenades, colleges, theatres, shops, railways and roads leading in all directions. Thus, by recognizing the right of Mr. So-and-So to a particular house in Paris, London or Rouen, the law is unjustly appropriating to him a certain portion of the produce of the labor of mankind in general. And it is precisely because this appropriation and all other forms of property bearing the same character are a crying injustice, that a whole arsenal of laws and a whole army of soldiers, policemen and judges are needed to maintain it against the good sense and just feeling inherent in humanity.

Half our laws,—the civil code in each country,—serves no other purpose than to maintain this appropriation, this monopoly for the benefit of certain individuals against the whole of mankind. Three-fourths of the causes decided by the tribunals are nothing but quarrels between monopolists—two robbers disputing over their booty. And a great many of our criminal laws have the same object in view, their end being to keep the workman in a subordinate position towards his employer, and thus afford security for exploitation.

As for guaranteeing the product of his labor to the producer, there are no laws which even attempt such a thing. It is so simple and natural, so much a part of the manners and customs of mankind, that law has not given it so much as a thought. Open brigandage, sword in hand, is no feature of our age. Neither does one workman ever come and dispute the produce of his labor with another. If they have a misunderstanding they settle it by calling in a third person, without having recourse to law. The only person who exacts from another what that other has produced, is the proprietor, who comes in and deducts the lion's share. As for humanity in general, it everywhere respects the right of each to what he has created, without the interposition of any special laws.

As all the laws about property which make up thick volumes of codes and are the delight of our lawyers have no other object than to protect the unjust appropriation of human labor by certain monopolists, there is no reason for their existence, and, on the day of the revolution, social revolutionists are thoroughly determined to put an end to them. Indeed, a bonfire might be made with perfect justice of all laws bearing upon the so-called "rights of property," all title-deeds, all registers, in a word, of all that is in any way connected with an institution which will soon be looked upon as a blot in the history of humanity, as humiliating as the slavery and serfdom of past ages.

The remarks just made upon laws concerning property are

quite as applicable to the second category of laws; those for the maintenance of government, i. e., constitutional law.

It again is a complete arsenal of laws, decrees, ordinances, orders in council, and what not, all serving to protect the diverse forms of representative government, delegated or usurped, beneath which humanity is writhing. We know very well—anarchists have often enough pointed out in their perpetual criticism of the various forms of government—that the mission of all governments, monarchical, constitutional, or republican, is to protect and maintain by force the privileges of the classes in possession, the aristocracy, clergy and traders. A good third of our laws—and each country possesses some tens of thousands of them—the fundamental laws on taxes, excise duties, the organization of ministerial departments and their offices, of the army, the police, the church, etc., have no other end than to maintain, patch up, and develop the administrative machine. And this machine in its turn serves almost entirely to protect the privileges of the possessing classes. Analyze all these laws, observe them in action day by day, and you will discover that not one is worth preserving.

About such laws there can be no two opinions. Not only anarchists, but more or less revolutionary radicals also, are agreed that the only use to be made of laws concerning the organization of government is to fling them into the fire.

The third category of law still remains to be considered; that relating to the protection of the person and the detection and prevention of "crime." This is the most important because most prejudices attach to it; because, if law enjoys a certain amount of consideration, it is in consequence of the belief that this species of law is absolutely indispensable to the maintenance of security in our societies. These are laws developed from the nucleus of customs useful to human communities, which have been turned to account by rulers to sanctify their own domination. The authority of the chiefs of tribes, of rich families in towns, and of the king, depended upon their judicial functions, and even down to the present day, whenever the necessity of government is spoken of, its function as supreme judge is the thing implied. "Without a government men would tear one another to pieces," argues the village orator. "The ultimate end of all government is to secure twelve honest jurymen to every accused person," said Burke.

Well, in spite of all the prejudices existing on this subject, it is quite time that anarchists should boldly declare this category of laws as useless and injurious as the preceding ones.

First of all, as to so-called "crimes"—assaults upon persons

—it is well known that two-thirds, and often as many as three-fourths, of such "crimes" are instigated by the desire to obtain possession of someone's wealth. This immense class of so-called "crimes and misdemeanors" will disappear on the day on which private property ceases to exist. "But," it will be said, "there will always be brutes who will attempt the lives of their fellow citizens, who will lay their hands to a knife in every quarrel, and revenge the slightest offense by murder, if there are no laws to restrain and punishments to withhold them." This refrain is repeated every time the right of society *to punish* is called in question.

Yet there is one fact concerning this head which at the present time is thoroughly established; the severity of punishment does not diminish the amount of crime. Hang, and, if you like, quarter murderers, and the number of murders will not decrease by one. On the other hand, abolish the penalty of death, and there will not be one murder more; there will be fewer. Statistics prove it. But if the harvest is good, and bread cheap, and the weather fine, the number of murders immediately decreases. This again is proved by statistics. The amount of crime always augments and diminishes in proportion to the price of provisions and the state of the weather. Not that all murders are actuated by hunger. That is not the case. But when the harvest is good, and provisions are at an obtainable price, and when the sun shines, men, lighter-hearted and less miserable than usual, do not give way to gloomy passions, do not from trivial motives plunge a knife into the bosom of a fellow creature.

Moreover, it is also a well known fact that the fear of punishment has never stopped a single murderer. He who kills his neighbor from revenge or misery does not reason much about consequences; and there have been few murderers who were not firmly convinced that they should escape prosecution.

Without speaking of a society in which a man will receive a better education, in which the development of all his faculties, and the possibility of exercising them, will procure him so many enjoyments that he will not seek to poison them by remorse—even in our society, even with those sad products of misery whom we see today in the public houses of great cities—on the day when no punishment is inflicted upon murderers, the number of murders will not be augmented by a single case. And it is extremely probable that it will be, on the contrary, diminished by all those cases which are due at present to habitual criminals, who have been brutalized in prisons.

We are continually being told of the benefits conferred by law, and the beneficial effect of penalties, but have the speakers ever attempted to strike a balance between the benefits attributed to laws and penalties, and the degrading effect of these penalties upon humanity? Only calculate all the evil passions awakened in mankind by the atrocious punishments formerly inflicted in our streets! Man is the cruelest animal upon earth. And who has pampered and developed the cruel instincts unknown, even among monkeys, if it is not the king, the judge, and the priests, armed with law, who caused flesh to be torn off in strips, boiling pitch to be poured into wounds, limbs to be dislocated, bones to be crushed, men to be sawn asunder to maintain their authority? Only estimate the torrent of depravity let loose in human society by the "informing" which is countenanced by judges, and paid in hard cash by governments, under pretext of assisting in the discovery of "crime." Only go into the jails and study what man becomes when he is deprived of freedom and shut up with other depraved beings, steeped in the vice and corruption which oozes from the very walls of our existing prisons. Only remember that the more these prisons are reformed, the more detestable they become. Our model modern penitentiaries are a hundred-fold more abominable than the dungeons of the middle ages. Finally, consider what corruption, what depravity of mind is kept up among men by the idea of obedience, the very essence of law; of chastisement; of authority having the right to punish, to judge irrespective of our conscience and the esteem of our friends; of the necessity for executioners, jailers, and informers—in a word, by all the attributes of law and authority. Consider all this, and you will assuredly agree with us in saying that a law inflicting penalties is an abomination which should cease to exist.

Peoples without political organization, and therefore less depraved than ourselves, have perfectly understood that the man who is called "criminal" is simply unfortunate; that the remedy is not to flog him, to chain him up, or to kill him on the scaffold or in prison, but to help him by the most brotherly care, by treatment based on equality, by the usages of life among honest men. In the next revolution we hope that this cry will go forth:

"Burn the guillotines; demolish the prisons; drive away the judges, policemen and informers—the impurest race upon the face of the earth; treat as a brother the man who has been led by passion to do ill to his fellow; above all, take from the ignoble products of middle-class idleness the possibility of displaying their vices in attractive colors; and be sure that but few crimes will mar our society."

The main supports of crime are idleness, law and authority; laws about property, laws about government, laws about penalties and misdemeanors; and authority, which takes upon itself to manufacture these laws and to apply them.

No more laws! No more judges! Liberty, equality, and practical human sympathy are the only effectual barriers we can oppose to the anti-social instincts of certain among us.

Bibliography

Legal Cases

146 In order to get an idea of how the American legal system responds to civil disobedience and related issues, the reader should consult the judicial opinions in the following recent representative cases:

Edwards v. South Carolina, 372 U.S. 229 (1963)

Cox. v. Louisiana, 379 U.S. 536 (1964)

Williams v. Wallace, 240 F. Supp. 100 (M.D. Ala. 1965)

Adderley v. Florida, 385 U.S. 39 (1966)

Walker v. City of Birmingham, 388 U.S. 307 (1967)

United States v. O'Brien, 391 U.S. 367 (1968)

Shuttlesworth v. City of Birmingham, 394 U.S. 147 (1969)

Gutknecht v. United States, 396 U.S. 295 (1970)

Gillette v. United States and *Negre v. Larsen et al.,* decided on March 8, 1971.

Further relevant cases will be found cited in the texts and notes of the above.

Just before this volume went to press, the Supreme Court decided (March 8, 1971) in *Gillette v. United States* that objection to a particular war, even if conscientious, does not constitute a sufficient ground for exemption from the obligation to serve in the armed forces. Only pacifism may so exempt. The opinions in this case would merit the reader's careful examination.

Books and Articles

Acton, H. B. "Political Justification," *Contemporary British Philosophy* (H. D. Lewis, ed.). London: Macmillan, 1956.

Allen, Francis. "Civil Disobedience and the Legal Order," *University of Cincinnati Law Review* (Winter 1967).

Arendt, Hannah. *On Violence.* New York: Harcourt Brace Jovanovich, 1970.

Bay, Christian. "Civil Disobedience," *International Encyclopedia of the Social Sciences.* New York: Macmillan, 1968.

Bayne, D. C. *Conscience, Obligation and the Law.* Chicago: Loyola University Press, 1966.

Bedau, Hugo Adam. "On Civil Disobedience," *Journal of Philosophy* (October 12, 1961).

——— (ed.). *Civil Disobedience: Theory and Practice.* New York: Pegasus, 1969.

Bennett, John C. "The Place of Civil Disobedience," *Christianity and Crisis* (December 25, 1967).

Black, Charles L., Jr. "The Problem of the Compatibility of Civil Disobedience with American Institutions of Government," *Texas Law Review,* Vol. 43 (1965).

Blackstone, W. T. "Civil Disobedience: Is It Justified?" *Georgia Law Review,* Vol. 3 (1969).

Brown, Stuart M., Jr. "Civil Disobedience," *Journal of Philosophy,* Vol. 58 (1961).

Brownell, Herbert. "Civil Disobedience—A Lawyer's Challenge," *American Criminal Law Quarterly* (Fall 1964).

Cameron, J. M. "On Violence," *New York Review of Books* (July 2, 1970).

Campbell, A. H. "Obligation and Obedience to Law," *Proceedings of the British Academy,* Vol. 51 (1965).

Camus, Albert. *The Rebel.* New York: Vintage, 1958.

Carnes, John R. "Why Should I Obey the Law?" *Ethics* (October 1960).

Caudwell, Christopher. "Pacifism and Violence: A Study in Bourgeois Ethics," *Studies and Further Studies in a Dying Culture.* New York: Dodd, Mead, 1938.

Chomsky, Noam, William Earle, and John R. Silber. "Philosophers and Public Policy: A Symposium," *Ethics* (October 1968).

Clark, Tom C. "Philosophy, Law, and Civil Disobedience," *Ethics and Social Justice* (Howard E. Kiefer and Milton K. Munitz, eds.). New York: New York University Press, 1968. This is a reply to Hughes' "Civil Disobedience and the Political Question Doctrine."

Cohen, Carl. "Essence and Ethics of Civil Disobedience," *The Nation* (March 16, 1964).

———. *Civil Disobedience.* New York: Columbia University Press, 1971.

Cohen, Marshall. "Civil Disobedience in a Constitutional Democracy," *Massachusetts Review* (Spring 1969).

Conant, Ralph W. "Rioting, Insurrection and Civil Disobedience," *The American Scholar* (Summer 1968).

Cox, Archibald, et al. *Civil Rights, the Constitution, and the Courts.* Cambridge, Mass.: Harvard University Press, 1967.

Dellinger, David. *Revolutionary Nonviolence.* New York: Doubleday, 1971.

Dickinson, John. "A Working Theory of Sovereignty," *Political Science Quarterly* (1928).

Douglas, William O. *Points of Rebellion.* New York: Vintage, 1969.

Dworkin, Ronald. "A Theory of Civil Disobedience," *Ethics and Social Justice* (Howard E. Kiefer and Milton K. Munitz, eds.). New York: New York University Press, 1968.

Fortas, Abe. *Concerning Dissent and Civil Disobedience.* New York: Signet (NAL), 1968.

Freeman, Harrop A., et al. *Civil Disobedience.* Santa Barbara: Center for the Study of Democratic Institutions, 1966.

Gandhi, Mohandas K. *Non-violent Resistance.* New York: Schocken Books, 1964.

Garver, Newton. "What Violence Is," *The Nation* (June 24, 1968).

Green, Thomas Hill. *Lectures on the Principles of Political Obligation.* London (1921).

Griswold, Erwin N. "Dissent—1968," *Tulane Law Review* (June 1968).

Grodzins, Morton. *The Loyal and the Disloyal: Social Boundaries of Patriotism and Treason.* Chicago: University of Chicago Press, 1956.

Hall, Robert T. "Legal Toleration of Civil Disobedience," *Ethics* (January 1971).

Harrison, Bernard. "Violence and the Rule of Law," *Violence* (Jerome Shaffer, ed.). New York: McKay, 1971.

Holmes, Robert L. "Violence and Nonviolence," *Violence* (Jerome Shaffer, ed.). New York: McKay, 1971.

Hook, Sidney (ed.). *Law and Philosophy.* New York: New York University Press, 1964. This volume contains several replies to the article "Legal Obligation and the Duty of Fair Play" by John Rawls.

Hughes, Graham. "Civil Disobedience and the Political Question Doctrine," *New York University Law Review* (March 1968).

Kant, Immanuel. "Concerning the Common Saying: This May Be True in Theory but Does Not Apply in Practice," *The Philosophy of Kant* (Carl J. Friedrich, ed.-trans.). New York: Random House, 1949.

————. *The Metaphysical Elements of Justice* (John Ladd, trans.). Indianapolis: Bobbs-Merrill, 1965, esp. pp. 84–89, 133–137.

Keeton, Morris. "The Morality of Civil Disobedience," *Texas Law Review* (March 1965).

Kelsen, Hans. "Why Should the Law Be Obeyed?" *What Is Justice?* Berkeley: University of California Press, 1957.

King, Martin Luther, Jr. "Letter from Birmingham City Jail," *Liberation* (June 1963).

————. "Love, Law and Civil Disobedience," *New South,* Vol. 16 (1961).

Laski, Harold. *The Dangers of Obedience.* New York: Harper & Row, 1930.

Lewis, H. D. "Obedience to Conscience," *Mind,* Vol. 54 (1945).

Lewy, Guenter. "Resistance to Tyranny," *Western Political Quarterly* (September 1960).

————. "Superior Orders, Nuclear Warfare, and the Dictates of Conscience," *American Political Science Review* (March 1961).

Liebman, Morris I. "Civil Disobedience—A Threat to Our Law Society," *American Criminal Law Quarterly* (Fall 1964).

Locke, John. *Two Treatises of Government* (Peter Laslett, ed.). Cambridge: Cambridge University Press, 1960. Though not himself elaborating a theory of civil disobedience, Locke sets out ideals and principles that are very often appealed to in justifications of civil disobedience.

Lynd, Staughton (ed.). *Non-violence in America.* Indianapolis: Bobbs-Merrill, 1966.

MacFarlane, Leslie J. "Justifying Political Disobedience," *Ethics* (October 1968).

McWilliams, Wilson Carey. "Civil Disobedience and Contemporary Constitutionalism: The American Case," *Comparative Politics* (January 1969).

Marcuse, Herbert. "The Problem of Violence and the Radical Opposition," *Five Lectures.* Boston: Beacon Press, 1970.

Martin, Rex. "Civil Disobedience," *Ethics* (January 1970).

Miller, William R. *Nonviolence: A Christian Interpretation.* New York: Association Press, 1966.

The Monist, Vol. 54, No. 4 (October 1970) is entirely devoted to the topics of legal obligation and civil disobedience.

Murphy, Jeffrie G. "Violence and the Rule of Law," *Ethics* (July 1970). This is a reply to Robert Paul Wolff's "On Violence."

Naess, Arne. *Gandhi and the Nuclear Age.* Totowa: Bedminster Press, 1964.

Narveson, Jan. "Pacifism: A Philosophical Analysis," *Ethics* (July 1965).

Neumann, Franz L. "On the Limits of Justifiable Disobedience," *Conflict of Loyalties* (R. M. MacIver, ed.). New York: Institute for Religious and Social Studies, 1952.

Nieburg, H. L. "The Ethics of Resistance to Tyranny," *American Political Review* (December 1962).

Ofstad, H. "The Ethics of Resistance to Tyranny," *Inquiry* (Autumn 1961).

Pennock, J. Roland, and John W. Chapman (eds.). *Nomos XII: Political and Legal Obligation.* New York: Atherton Press, 1970.

Pitkin, Hannah. "Obligation and Consent," *American Political Science Review* (1965).

Power, Paul F. "On Civil Disobedience in Recent American Democratic Thought," *American Political Science Review* (March 1970).

Prosch, Harry. "Toward an Ethics of Civil Disobedience," *Ethics* (April 1967).

Rawls, John. "The Justification of Civil Disobedience," *Civil Disobedience: Theory and Practice* (Hugo Adam Bedau, ed.). New York: Pegasus, 1969.

Riehm, John W. "Civil Disobedience—A Definition," *American Criminal Law Quarterly* (Fall 1964).

Rostow, Eugene V. "No Right to Civil Disobedience," *Trial* (June–July 1970).

Rucker, Darnell. "The Moral Grounds of Civil Disobedience," *Ethics* (January 1966).

Russell, Bertrand. "Civil Disobedience," *New Statesman* (February 17, 1961).

Sibley, Mulford Q. "On Political Obligation and Civil Disobedience," *Journal of the Minnesota Academy of Science* (1965).

———— (ed.). *The Quiet Battle: Writings on the Theory and Practice of Non-violent Resistance.* New York: Doubleday, 1963.

————. *The Obligation to Disobey.* New York: Council on Religion and International Affairs, 1970.

Sorel, Georges. *Reflections on Violence.* New York: Macmillan, 1950.

Spitz, David. "Democracy and the Problem of Civil Disobedience," *Essays in the Liberal Idea of Freedom.* Tucson: University of Arizona Press, 1964.

Spock, Benjamin. "Vietnam and Civil Disobedience," *The Humanist* (January–February 1968).

Sturzo, Luigi. "The Right to Rebel," *Dublin Review* (1937).

Van den Haag, Ernest. "Government, Conscience, and Disobedience," *Sidney Hook and the Contemporary World* (Paul Kurtz, ed.). New York: John Day Co., 1968.

Van Dusen, Lewis H., Jr. "Civil Disobedience: Destroyer of Democracy," *American Bar Association Journal* (February 1969).

Walzer, Michael. "The Obligation to Disobey," *Ethics* (April 1967). Also in *Political Theory and Social Change* (David Spitz, ed.). New York: Atherton Press, 1967.

————. "Corporate Authority and Civil Disobedience," *Dissent* (September–October 1969).

————. *Obligations: Essays on Disobedience, War, and Citizenship.* Cambridge, Mass.: Harvard University Press, 1970.

Wasserstrom, Richard A. "Disobeying the Law," *Journal of Philosophy* (October 12, 1961).

————. "The Obligation to Obey the Law," *U.C.L.A. Law Review* (1963). Also in *Essays in Legal Philosophy* (Robert S. Summers, ed.). Berkeley: University of California Press, 1968.

Whittaker, Charles E., and William Sloane Coffin, Jr. *Law, Order and Civil Disobedience.* Washington, 1967.

Wofford, Harris, Jr. "Non-violence and the Law," *Journal of Religious Thought,* 1957.

Wolff, Robert Paul. "On Violence," *Journal of Philosophy* (October 2, 1969).

Woozley, A. D. "Socrates on Disobeying the Law," *Socrates* (Gregory Vlastos, ed.). New York: Doubleday, 1971.

Zahn, Gordon. *War, Conscience and Dissent.* New York: Hawthorn, 1967.